LUN~ ...._ ..... _~...

"[Katherine McGraw Patterson] lays out a series of pithy observations and tips for people in the business world...[who] will find an enormous amount of worthy advice in these pages. A fun and demystifying manual that seeks to humanize networking."

- Kirkus Reviews

"[Katherine McGraw Patterson] shares her own journey of overcoming her aversion to networking to subsequently leading one of Denver's fastest-growing professional networks for women business owners... People will be using this book as a tool to expand their networks for a long time."

- Dr. Ivan Misner, Founder of BNI and
New York Times Bestselling Author

"[Katherine McGraw Patterson] helps readers overcome their fear of networking by delving into the why, where, and how of getting out there and making connections...Every small business owner should read this book."

- Molly Gimmel, CEO of Design To Delivery Inc and
Board Chair, National Association of Women Business Owners

"[Katherine McGraw Patterson] shares her networking experiences in a candid, practical and easy to read fashion allowing you to learn and grow through applying the 'How To's' with a strategy designed for your success."

- Tammy Urbach, 4BR CEO & Founder

LUNCHING WITH LIONS

LUNCHING WITH LIONS

STRATEGIES FOR THE
NETWORKING-AVERSE

by Katherine McGraw Patterson

TWO CHICKENS PRESS · EST 2018

Lunching with Lions: Strategies for the Networking-Averse
Published by Two Chickens Press
Broomfield, CO

ISBN: 978-0-578-43847-4

BUSINESS DEVELOPMENT / Entrepreneurship

QUANTITY PURCHASES: Schools, companies, professional groups, clubs, and other organizations may qualify for special terms when ordering quantities of this title. For information, email hello@twochickenspress.com.

Book design by Katherine McGraw Patterson

COVER QUOTE:
According to my attempts to identify the original source, no one person can lay claim to this modern proverb. It's been attributed to a number of politicians and public figures over the years, but it seems generally accepted that it first originated in Washington, D.C. sometime around 2000.

Dedicated to all the entrepreneurs and small business owners who wake up every day and do the things that scare them most in pursuit of their vision.

TABLE OF CONTENTS

HOW I BECAME THE PROFESSIONAL NEW GIRL

17 + 7 + 4 + 39 = 20

As my bestie and I always say, "Damn the maths!"

Let me break those numbers down for you, friend....

Seventeen cities. Seven states. Four countries. Thirty-nine different residences. It all adds up to 20 major moves in my lifetime. Twenty moves. People, I was born in 1968, so if you're still doing the math, that means that as I sit and write this, I've moved, on average, every two and a half years for *my entire life.*

Hi. I'm Katherine, and I'm a Professional New Girl.

My story usually starts with me saying something like, "We moved around a bit when I was growing up." (Oh, yeah. I'm a master of understatement.) My listener will usually ask, "Oh, was your dad in the military?" That's the point at which I launch into a long-winded explanation of how my father was an idealist, always searching for the perfect job, and how we relocated from place to place until my middle-school years, when he finally bought his own business back in the ancestral homeland, Texas.

When I tell people about my transient upbringing, I try to keep it light and entertaining. It's my go-to party trick. What that glib little rehearsed story doesn't cover—because it's just too raw for me still—is the fact that all those moves, and the six different schools I attended before college, were tough. They were more than tough. They sucked.

Sure, eventually I made friends wherever we landed. And I met people from all types of economic and social backgrounds. The elementary school I attended in Tennessee was 80 percent African-American, as was my Brownie Troop. My friends in West Virginia were legit hillbillies with dads who were coal miners, who lived "up the holler" and only came to town during the week for school. No high school football games, roller skating, or movies on the square for them. Our New Jersey town was a suburb of New York City, where my classmates were the scions of Wall Street stockbrokers and (it was rumored) fathers "connected" to the mob, and who fell mainly into one of three ethnicities: Jewish, Irish Catholic, or Italian. Then, it was back to Texas and the Dallas suburbs, where old money mingled with new and my classmates popped the collars on their Ralph Lauren Polos and cuffed the hems of their madras plaid Bermuda shorts before they left for the country club.

This exposure to so many different kinds of people and regional traditions certainly made me more accepting of others, more adaptable, and a greater lover of travel. But.

I never really fit in. Not completely.

As an adult, when I would tell the story of my transient childhood, I used the term "Professional New Girl," which I'd coined to describe the unique skill set my upbringing brought me. As a Professional New Girl, I had to learn to read the social situation quickly. I had to adapt to new cultural mores fast if I wanted to make friends (survive) in my new environment.

I learned how to be "on," how to be a social chameleon, and how to read a room fast. I learned how to fake confidence, how to tell my story over and over and over again, and how to wade through the shallow end of friendship (that tentative getting-to-know-you/are-we-a-good-fit stage) to the deeper end of true relationships. How to smile even when I wanted to crawl into my bed and cry for my last home, my last set of friends, the last place I felt I belonged.

As I write this, I'm jokingly calling it my trauma narrative because it was traumatic (albeit, trauma with a little t). I can't discount that fact. It sucked rocks to always be the new girl, always having to try on new friendships and new cultures. And, it left lasting emotional scars.

The way those scars show up today is that I hate networking. Every time I walk into a new networking situation, the story in my head is that everyone in the room already knows everyone else and that I'm the outsider. Even the word "networking" conjures up a visual of a room full of people's backs, and poor little me, tapping shoulders, trying to get their attention while they laugh and share inside jokes among themselves. The mental image is of a big, scary room full of unfriendly strangers. Ugh. Damage.

That was the story I told myself for years. And I created a way to do business around it. I worked really, really hard for a really, really long time to build a business that didn't require me to network. I aligned myself with organizations and other businesses that could direct projects and clients my way without me ever having to go out and connect. I worked with clients remotely—never locally—so that I had an excuse to avoid those uncomfortable networking situations.

Then came a time when I completely changed my business focus, and I realized I had to get out and build my local connections if I wanted to succeed. And all the junk I had around networking came bubbling to the surface. Not only did I have to change how I was doing things, I had to change my story too.

I took a long look at my relationships, both personal and business, and I started to realize that, although the story in my head was that I hated networking, in reality, I was really, really good at it. I'm a natural connector. All those years of needing to make friends, create connections, and find my social standing immediately in order to survive paid off. While I'm still painfully, tragically uncomfortable walking into a room full of strangers, I can do it, and I can do it well. I have a strong handshake and engaging smile, and I like to talk to people about themselves. I'm a natural tribe builder. Shoot, I was PTA president two years after moving to my kids' newest—perhaps last (Oh, please God, let it be the last!)—school. Yes, obviously, I have "sucker" tattooed on my forehead. But still, I knew no one when we arrived, and two years later, I had enough of a tribe that I was elevated to the ultimate social position in an upper-middle-class elementary school. Am I "popular"? I don't know what that means when you're 50. But I have people.

I digress. When I shook up my business, I knew I'd also have to shake up my paradigm in order to succeed. That meant no more hiding in my office, but actually getting out and connecting with the people who could help me grow my business. So, I created a personal networking challenge. I set a goal for the number of groups I'd visit and the number of one-on-one coffees I'd have each week. I consciously examined the types of networking groups available and evaluated which were the right ones for me and my goals. I tracked my results. I took some emotional and personal risks in how I connected with people, and I learned a boatload about networking. I treated it like a business project and took my emotions out of it. I basically forced myself to pull up my big girl panties, smile, and get out there.

The biggest thing I learned is that we're not actually ever taught how to network. Oh, sure, we know we *should* network—because we're told to and because people all around us are doing it—but we're never really shown *how*.

This book shares with you the skills I've learned over a lifetime of being a Professional New Girl as well as the lessons I learned in the past few years about how to be a better networker for your business.

INTRODUCTION

Picture this: The sun rises above the swaying grasses of the prehistoric savannah, and there, in the distance, a tiny tribe of pre-people is traveling as a group for protection. As they move across the grasslands, animals are approaching. The beasts grow closer, and the pre-people begin to move more quickly, headed for a large rock outcropping. Suddenly, from the top of the rocks, two arms thrust a tiny lion cub upwards, its face toward the sun. The pre-people see the animals kneel and hear them begin to sing "It's the circle of life..."

Oops, sorry. Wrong story.

Let's go back to the little band of our prehistoric ancestors. The land around them is vast and wild, and the dangers are real. Within the tribe, mothers work together to care for all the children, and the hunters venture out to provide food for the entire group. Young men protect the women and children from harm. Together, the band watches out for and shelters all its members, making sure they're safe and secure.

Except for Bob.

Bob joined our little tribe recently after leaving another group due to an unfortunate incident with the leader's daughter, a mango, and a baboon. He hasn't been with our tiny band of pre-people for long. He hasn't hunted with the men. He doesn't eat with the rest of the group, preferring to sit quietly by himself and eat the foods he brought with him when he arrived. He doesn't offer to share any of his supplies. Bob also declined to watch the tribe's tiniest pre-humans when the women wanted a night off to go eat fermented berries. Bob pretty much keeps to himself.

Which is why, when Bob trips, sprains his ankle, and is unable to keep up with the tribe on the trek across the grasslands, no one notices. The distance between the group and Bob grows as he hobbles to catch up. Eventually, the little band disappears over the horizon, and Bob is alone. From somewhere nearby, Bob hears a lion roar.

Poor Bob.

Although modern humans don't have to worry about being eaten by lions on a daily basis, we are the great-great-great-great-great-great-great-great-great-great-great-great-great-great-great-great-great-grandchildren of that little tribe of pre-people (except for Bob, who was lion lunch before he could make any mini-Bobs), and we're genetically hardwired to form the relationships we need for protection against threats.

But, evolution is a cruel, cruel trickster. On the one hand, she created the drive in us to form relationships in order to protect ourselves. On the other, she created an opposite and contrary fear: the fear of strangers.

Identifying with and belonging to a group is healthy and necessary, but it can also lead to a primal suspicion of those who don't belong. Primate studies show that our chimpanzee cousins have an acute awareness of who's "in" and who's "out" when it comes to resources. We've evolved a kind of natural protectiveness of the interests of the group as well as a corresponding drive to eliminate threats to those interests. This natural protectiveness can cause members to shun those who are perceived as a danger.[1]

Add to that the social conditioning we experience as children. We're taught not to talk to strangers. In fact, we're taught to fear strangers. Sure, as we grow and learn to discern people's intentions, we can override that training. But it's still there, lurking, and it can show up the minute we walk into a room full of people we don't know. We're strangers to them, they're strangers to us. It's a mess.

As a result, we humans have developed a kind of hyper-awareness that gives us the profound ability to interpret the thoughts and feelings of the people we interact with. This "mindreading" is what allows us to cooperate and collaborate with others, letting us decipher their motivations and adjust our own behaviors accordingly.

If we're in the group and approached from the outside, our primal guard goes up, and our lizard brain starts scanning for signs of threat from the outsider. The outsider, on the other hand, is scrutinizing members of the group for signs of acceptance (best case) or hostility (worst case).

Belonging to a group is predicated on the goodwill of others, and we've evolved an innate hyper-sensitivity to what is socially acceptable. It's that sensitivity that researchers think lies at the root of social anxiety. We're constantly battling a subconscious angst about whether our actions are okay or offensive, whether we'll be brought into the tribe or banished. Our social anxiety is actually keeping us attuned to the "rules of the game" so that we earn the goodwill of the group and find our place quickly.

Brain scans show that we have two different systems in our brains to support social and nonsocial thinking, and that they work in tandem.[2] As one part of the brain is engaged, the other takes a back seat, and vice versa. When we're dealing with an analytical problem, the social thinking part of our brain takes a break. But as soon as we solve the nonsocial problem, the social thinking part of our brain comes back online. The theory is that this wiring allows us to deduce the thoughts and intents behind the actions we see from others. Evolution has prepared us to succeed and survive by constantly interpreting the world from this social viewpoint, minimizing the risk of being left behind. Like Bob.

Being excluded—either by intention or because you lack a social group—can have lasting, damaging consequences. Studies show that the emotional effects of being ostracized, even by strangers, even for a short amount of time, triggers the same areas of the brain as physical pain. Researchers have also found that just *imagining* the possibility of being left out will cause psychological agony.[3]

To recap, we're constantly juggling our fear of meeting new people with the fear of being alone.

Humans. Are. A. Hot. Mess.

When I was honing my skills as a Professional New Girl, I had to learn to balance—and overcome—the fear of meeting new people with the driving need to assimilate into the group for survival. Imagine poor little me, in kindergarten, in fourth grade, in the *middle* of sixth grade (ugh, thanks, Mom and Dad), and as a freshman in high school, walking into a situation where I knew no one. For weeks at a time, literally every person I encountered was a stranger. I experienced that physical and emotional pain of being excluded, because my peers were just as leery about accepting me and having someone new enter the group (red alert: stranger in our midst!) as I was about finding my place. And, yes, that pain had lasting consequences.

Which is why, if you'd asked me a few years ago, I would have vehemently stated that I hated networking. *Hated. It.* The fear and distress I felt about walking into a room full of strangers was real for me. Very real. As a result, I worked really, really hard for a really, really long time to build a business that didn't require me to network. Eventually, however, my business grew and changed, and the need to build a larger network grew and changed too.

As an elementary, middle, and high school student, success and belonging looked like having someone to eat lunch with, share homework with, and walk home with. It meant having girlfriends to go roller skating with, to tell me my new Farrah Fawcett hairdo was cool, to gossip about boys with. Success and survival simply meant having people.

Today, as a business owner, survival means so much more. Yes, the social relationships are still vital, but now success means a steady income to support my family, new clients to create that income, and partners who can help me grow my business. Success means creating a strong and varied network of other business owners, peer advisors, clients, and community members who will "watch out" for me and my business and keep me from getting eaten by the proverbial lions.

The financial stakes of networking are much higher as a business owner than as a teenager, and yet the social anxiety and fear of being left out are just as real in both cases.

Basically, I'm here to tell you that networking can be hard and awkward, and it can push you out of your comfort zone. That pasting a smile on your face and wading into a room full of strangers can be terrifying. That it's okay if you've held back from engaging in business networking due to those fears. Because I've been there.

I'm also here to tell you that you can overcome those anxieties—that you can build your networking "muscle" through practice and repetition. I'm going to show you that when you create awareness, purpose, and intent around your networking, you can create systems, scripts, and strategies that help you feel in control and alleviate some of the negative emotions around it. And when you eliminate those emotions, you can become a networking superstar.

How can I promise you these outcomes? Because I did it. I went from someone who *hated* networking to someone who can walk up to a stranger and walk away 15 minutes later with that person's business card and a coffee date. And enjoy doing it. I've built my networking skills so well that when I tell people now how much I used to loathe and fear it, they laugh. They can't imagine that I—who (apparently) glides so (seemingly) effortlessly through networking events—ever had any challenges with it at all. (Note: I say "apparently" and "seemingly" because, while on the outside I look as if I've got this sh*t conquered, in reality, I still face networking fears every day. But I'm able to do it anyway because of the techniques and strategies I'll share in this book.)

Where's the proof that I've tackled at least some of my challenges? In September 2016, on a whim, I started a social media group for women entrepreneurs. At the time, I was going through my own personal networking challenge (more on that later), and connecting online was one of the steps on my list. When I created the group, I figured I'd get 10 to 15 women I already knew who might, occasionally, be interested in discussing our businesses. Within a month, I had 120 members. Three months later, we were holding regular monthly in-person events such as lunches and trainings. Today, WEBO Network has over 600 group members, a paid membership of nearly 100, a partnership with Colorado's largest regional chamber of commerce, and a robust calendar of networking events, professional development, mastermind groups, and other activities.

All because I was able to make and leverage connections. Something my people call "networking."

Throughout this book, I'll point you to additional resources you can use on the LunchingWithLions.com website to assist you with networking skills, such as honing your elevator speech, as well as tracking and nurturing your networking contacts and activities. These resources are free for you to use, so please do!

Take it from me, the Professional New Girl: you can do this. You can become the bomb-diggity of networking. Stick with me. I'll show you how.

HELLO
my name is

Chapter 1

IT'S NOT SALES

et me tell you about the time I almost got eaten by lions.
When I was just getting started in my business, I asked my dad (also an entrepreneur) how I should go about making some connections to support my growth. He suggested joining a networking or leads group. Since the word "networking" gave me the willies at the time, I decided on the latter.

A few weeks after I joined a leads group at a local chamber of commerce, one of the gentlemen in the group asked me to coffee to "learn more about what I did." I'm embarrassed to say it now, but my first thought was, "Hot damn! He's going to hire me to do his marketing. This networking stuff is paying off already!"

Um, not so much.

I eagerly showed up at the coffee date, portfolio in hand. We talked. And talked. We laughed. He asked lots of questions about me, whereas I (I'm ashamed to say) didn't do a very good job of asking him *anything* about his business. Honestly, he seemed pretty interested in my work. But, to my disappointment, he never quite got around to asking me to work for him. WTF?

In the days and weeks that followed, as I waited for him to suddenly realize he'd forgotten to ask me for pricing or a proposal, I went over our coffee date in my head. I thought about it from all angles. Why had he asked me so many questions if he wasn't interested in working together? Why had he asked me with whom I preferred to work? Why had we gone to coffee at all?

The more I thought about it, the more I came to realize that he had not, in fact, asked me to coffee in order to interview me. Or, rather, he was interviewing me, but not for a job. He was interviewing me as a *contact* in his network. He was getting to know me and my business, understanding where I fit into his world, and from that understanding, how he could best support my goals.

Suffice to say, I learned a big lesson from that coffee-that-was-just-a-coffee-and-not-a-job-offer: Networking is about connecting with other professionals and growing a—(wait for it)—network. It's not a sales call. If it were, we'd call it a sales call. It's not an interview. If it were—well, you get the picture.

As small-business owners, we're often told we *should* be networking to grow our business. (First of all, don't let people *should* all over you, but more about that later.) To many of us, "growing" is code for "increased profits," and because profits rely on sales, the unspoken implication is that networking will somehow generate the sales we need to succeed. It's no surprise, then, that a lot of business owners make the leap from that to the assumption that "networking" is, in fact, another word for "sales."

Nothing could be further from the truth.

For argument's sake, though, let's say networking is the same as sales.

If networking were sales, then when we walked into a new networking group of, say, 12 people, we'd look at each person around that table as a potential sale. And, for argument's sake, let's say you made all 12 sales. Congratulations!

Now what?

You've exhausted the sales potential of that group, and you're back to where you started, needing to make more sales in order to grow.

Now look at the same group of 12 people through the lens of networking.

Networking is about building relationships. I like to view it like dating. Unless you're on a reality TV show, you wouldn't go on a first date and expect to be engaged by the time the check arrived. You'd expect to get to know that person, spend time with that person, and see if you're compatible and if you have shared interests before you make a greater commitment.

Just like dating, networking isn't about making the sale the first time you meet someone. It's about building a relationship and mutual regard. And, in the same way that you wouldn't date someone you didn't want to spend time with, people don't want to do business with people they don't know, like, and trust.

LET THEM GET TO KNOW YOU

Great networkers know that in order to build solid relationships that pay off in referrals, partnerships, or (yes) sales, they have to put in consistent, sustained effort. That means finding the right group for you and your business goals, maintaining a presence, and building relationships within that group.

Too many times, I see business owners start networking only when they have a program or product to sell. They show up at a group where they're a newcomer (red alert: stranger in our midst!), they introduce themselves, and they pitch their offer. Then, they go to the next group, and the next, and the next. They're not networking. They're selling.

In my experience, they're not selling very well using this approach.

People get to know you when you show up. We've already talked about the evolutionary fear of strangers that humans carry around. How long does it take to make a friend? How many times do you have to meet someone before they become part of your tribe? Every time you give your introduction, every conversation they have with you, every question you answer helps them understand more about who you are, creates a stronger bond, and builds a deeper relationship.

BE LIKEABLE

Think about how you naturally connect to other people in your life and how you can translate that to building a professional relationship. Want my first and best advice on how to be likeable? Ask questions and focus on the other person.

Questions help uncover common interests, and they make the person you're with feel good. When you show genuine interest in someone, they feel valued and important, which makes them feel good, and it generates the goodwill that will help foster your connection. We all like it when someone shows sincere interest in us. And when someone likes you, they want to help you. That regard is what will help build a successful business relationship.

Asking questions opens the conversation. We've all met that person who verbally vomits all over us the first time we meet them. They're so intent on telling you about themselves, their business, their successes, and their dog that they don't seem to spare a second to consider you or your input.

Don't be that person.

Maybe I'm scarred from that disastrous coffee-that-was-just-a-coffee-and-not-a-job-offer, and I have lingering embarrassment over not showing interest in my coffee-date-who-was-not-going-to-be-my-client, but today I actually go into events and meetings planning not to talk about myself *at all*. It sounds extreme, but what I've found is that by not having an agenda about what I want to say and by completely focusing on the other person, when I do speak in response to something they've said, it feels authentic and genuine—which further nurtures the sense of connection between us.

EARN THEIR TRUST

Recently, I've been reading reports that trust is at an all-time low. Research shows that nearly one in five millennials believes "most people can't be trusted."[4] Ouch.

It's little wonder that trust between people is wavering. From Nigerian princes to catfishing scams, from fake Twitter profiles to "fake news," we just don't know what's real anymore. We can't even trust the perfect versions of our friends' lives that we see in our news feeds every day. They show us a carefully curated view of the perfect vacations, and the gorgeous homes, and the brilliant children—but not the reality of the crushing debt, the foreclosure notices, or the marital strife.

That *distrust* is bleeding over into our business relationships. People are worried about being scammed, taken advantage of, or just not treated right. It's our job as business owners to earn their trust, their business, and their referrals.

One of my favorite ways to build goodwill and trust is to offer something without strings attached. I try to find ways of being useful to my contact. Instead of thinking, "How can this person help me? What am I getting out of this meeting?" I focus on "Who do I know with whom I can connect her? How can I support her business?"

Sometimes that support and helpfulness looks as simple as an article that might be relevant. Maybe it's a recipe (seriously, common interests!). Other times, I might make an introduction to someone who could be a good connection. I've even gone so far as to offer some of my proprietary tools and resources—for free—because I felt that they might be useful to my contact.

I always, always try to offer something because it's a beautiful reason to continue the conversation past a coffee date. Which leads me to...deliver what you promise!

DELIVER WHAT YOU PROMISE

Follow-up is key. If I offer something during a networking engagement, I make a note of it (Professional New Girl Tip No. 142: always carry a notebook), and I follow up with an email thanking them for their time, and I include any links, introductions, tools, or recipes I want them to have.

Again, the offer, the delivery, and the prompt follow-up show your contacts that they're important to you, and these build on the goodwill that you've already worked so hard to establish.

Most importantly, show them that you are reliable, trust-worthy, and true to your word in all your dealings. After all, whether they're interviewing you as a contact, or they're inter-viewing you for a job, how you show up before, during, and after a networking engagement gives them a clue as to how you show up in your business as well. Be the kind of person and business they would be proud to recommend to their contacts.

Let's go back to those 12 people at your networking group. When you look at them as relationships, instead of sales, you expand your potential exponentially. Growing your professional network *amplifies* your brand. Your professional contacts can re-fer you to their network, market your programs and offers as affil-iates, facilitate introductions to people you're targeting, hook you up with valuable contacts, and so much more.

Consider this. The average person knows 600 people.[5] When we take that into consideration, those 12 people at the table become a network of 7,200 people. That's 7,200 people who might want to buy your product or service or 7,200 people who might want to invest in your business. Or 7,200 people who might provide referrals to their networks. (Wow, now we're up to 4,320,000 people!)

The point is, you never know where the relationships you build through networking might lead you and your business. If you look at the 12 people around the table as sales, then they're just 12 people. If you look at them as relationships, then they be-come an infinite number of possibilities.

Prompts and Activities

- Start a list of networking groups in your area. Note their meetings times and the investment for membership. Consider which you can commit to on a regular basis so that you can show up and establish a presence.

- Create a library of resources that reflect your philosophy, service, and brand (articles, tools, podcasts, influencers, etc.). Keep them in your back pocket as resources you can offer your contacts.

A FOUR-STEP BEGINNER'S GUIDE FOR THE NETWORKING-AVERSE
(OR: HOW KP LEARNED TO LOVE NETWORKING)

Every day, we create stories in our heads. Stories about ourselves, the people around us, and the world we live in. And you know what's crazy? We believe these stories are real because (let's be honest) we can come up with some doozies! The stories we make up are so much richer, more imaginative, and more dramatic than reality, it's as if we've created our own Thursday-night lineup and we just. Can't. Stop. Binge-watching.

It's little wonder that the story in my head about how much I hated networking had such a vice-like hold on me for so long. In fact, I built an entire business around the notion that I would not, could not ever be someone who had to network in order to succeed. Nope. Not me.

But then...

Flash back a couple years ago to a conversation I had with an acquaintance about my acute aversion to networking. Timing was everything here, folks, because this convo took place just as I was on the cusp of pivoting my business and I was distraught over the prospect of having to (gasp!) leave my happy little solitary home office and mingle with the masses.

The conversation with my friend was an epiphany for me. Here's how it went:

Me: I hate networking.

Bringer of the Epiphany: Well, then, how do you get most of your clients?

Me: Oh, I work with an organization that introduces me to its members.

Bringer of the Epiphany: How did you become involved in that organization?

Me: My previous boss introduced me to the organization's directors with a recommendation.

Bringer of the Epiphany: *raises eyebrow*

Me: ...

Well. There you have it. Simple words, huge impact. That story in my head kept me from seeing the truth. I'd convinced myself that I hated networking so thoroughly and completely that I *didn't even know I was doing it!* Many (most) of my past and current clients and engagements haven't come from marketing or advertising, but through relationships. And that's what networking is—building mutually beneficial connections and relationships.

This revelation that I was, in fact and in ignorance, networking quite nicely (after all, I've had a viable and successful business since 1999) came at a really opportune time. Thanks, Universe! I was refocusing my business in a way that absolutely would not, could not succeed without building connections to other local business owners. I couldn't keep covering my eyes and refusing to network. Nope, I had to pull up my big girl panties and get out there. I had to shake that proverbial moneymaker for everyone to see.

Was I happy about it? No. It scared me sh*tless. But understanding that the story wasn't true strengthened my resolve that the fear was something I could work through.

After that conversation, plus a few more with various other friends, and some pep talks from my dad (and maybe a cocktail or two) I reframed the story in my head. My existing "mindjunk" about networking being all about big, scary rooms full of strangers who weren't friendly just wasn't true. The reality is that I like people. My friends know that my motto is "the more the merrier." I connect with people and make new friends easily. After all, I'm the Professional New Girl!

It was as if the light bulb went on. Networking is about relationships. Relationships are about people. I like people. Therefore...I can like networking?

Whoa.

I mentioned earlier that this book would help you create strategies and systems that would help you become a networking ninja. I'm confident about this because I did it for myself. But, I had to start somewhere.

Just as I was kinda-sorta getting comfortable with the idea that I could change my mindjunk about networking, I realized I flat out didn't know how to do it (I've actually come to realize that most of us don't really know how to do it). So, what did I do? I did what any good strategist would do and gave myself some homework that would push my boundaries a bit. I created a strategy for my networking efforts, and now I'm sharing that strategy with you!

Here's my patented Four-Step Beginner's Guide for the Networking-Averse (just kidding about the patent, but it is a great place to start your own networking plan).

STEP 1. REFRAME YOUR STORY

What's your mindjunk around networking? You must have some, or you wouldn't have picked up this book. Are you hung up on the time commitment? The financial investment? Do you believe that your elevator speech isn't good enough? That there are too many coaches/mortgage brokers/sloth herders/(fill in your industry here) in all the networking groups already, so no one will notice you? That networking is big room full of scary, not-friendly strangers?

I'm a huge endorser of the Law of Attraction, which (simply put) says that what we put out into the Universe is what we get back. Therefore, if I stuck to my story that I hated networking, it was going to be—a hateful endeavor.

In order to change that reality, I had to change my story. Instead of telling myself how much I hated walking into a room full of strangers, I flipped my script. The truth is that I love meeting new people. I love to collect personalities and add them to my tribe. I'm a natural connector, and I get the tingles when I can put two people together in a way that helps them both. I reframed my story and created positive affirmations about my ability to network successfully. It sounds simple, but affirmations and the stories we tell ourselves have real power over our behaviors.

Whatever it is, get clear on the story you're telling yourself that's keeping you from being a master networker. Then, create the story you want to replace it with.

How will you reframe your story?

STEP 2. REACH OUT TO YOUR EXISTING FRIENDS

I'm going to go out on a limb here and assume you have friends. People who like you. People who want to see you succeed. Here's a tip: start networking with *them* first.

Oh, sure, you know what they do, and they know what you do, and if they were going to buy from you, they probably already would have.

But, have they shared your business with *their* friends and family? Have you asked them for referrals or introductions to their networks? Remember, the average human knows 600 other humans. If you haven't asked your friends and family for introductions or referrals, you haven't even scratched the surface of your existing network.

Surprisingly, reaching out to my friends and asking for introductions was the most emotionally vulnerable part of my whole personal networking challenge. If I was talking to strangers and I embarrassed myself, no one would have to know. But, if I was connecting with my friend's friend or business colleague and I crossed some sort of real or imaginary social line, yikes! Here come the lions!

One of my favorite quotes is attributed to John Burroughs. He said, "Leap and the net will appear." I took that to heart when I did the thing that scared me and made me feel incredibly exposed—I asked.

I sent out an email to my crew stating my desire to connect with women entrepreneurs and business owners. Those friends who I knew fit the bill got a personal invitation to sit down over coffee and share our stories. All of them got a request for referrals to their friends and a promise that I wouldn't abuse the favor by being pushy-salesy with any introductions. *And I let myself be vulnerable by sharing how hard it was for me to ask.* My friends were kind, supportive, and generous with names.

The next step was to reach out to the 30 or so names that were referred to me. The emails were simple. I mentioned our mutual acquaintance, explained that I wanted to connect with other women in business, and that, ultimately, I wanted to hear their stories about how they started their businesses and what challenges they face as women entrepreneurs. Then, I invited them to meet for coffee.

I'll be honest. Not everyone accepted my invitation or even responded to my emails. I didn't take it personally. After all, they didn't know me. And you know what? Every email I sent out got easier, and every coffee date got more comfortable. It's definitely a skill that can be learned and a muscle that can be strengthened. When I compare how intimidated I was to ask my own friends for introductions then to how many strangers I invite to engage in one-on-ones today, it blows my mind.

I'll say it again. If *I* can do this, *you* can do this!

STEP 3. NETWORK ONLINE

Quick. How many connections do you have on LinkedIn? How many of those are past coworkers or clients with whom you haven't corresponded in a while? What if you reached out to each of them (people you already know) and brought them up to speed on what you're doing? Reintroducing yourself to people who already know you and are familiar with you in a professional sense is a no-brainer way to jump-start your networking.

If you're a local business, using Facebook is another great way to connect with your potential clients. When I was challenging myself to up my networking game, I joined a few groups for moms and professional women. The beauty of these online groups is that they can be hyper-local, allowing you to build your reputation in the geographic area that you're focused on.

Regardless of where you choose to network online, whether it's LinkedIn, Facebook, Instagram, Twitter, or another industry niche site, the key is to be present and involved in the discussion.

I'll share more concrete tips for networking online in a later chapter, but the biggie is to *show up*—just like in-person networking, showing up gives people the chance to get to know you. Once I had reintroduced myself to my existing connections on LinkedIn, I started posting content and articles a few times a week. I also made sure to engage when my connections were posting by liking or commenting on their content.

Ditto on Facebook. I began to contribute regularly to the conversations in the groups I joined, offering suggestions and advice that were relevant to my business and authentic to my personality.

The relative anonymity of online networking makes it a lot easier for people who are nervous in face-to-face situations. But as with anything, you have to put in the effort to make it pay off.

STEP 4. NETWORK IN PERSON

Yes, you knew we'd get here. While it would be nice to stick with the people you already know in person and online, you're going to have to get out there and show your face in the right groups and events if you want to get real results.

I'll tell you what I've told my kids when they had to start at new schools after a move. That school is filled with your friends— you just haven't met them yet.

Corny? Yes.

True? Absolutely.

If networking in person triggers your mindjunk, just remember that every friend you have was a stranger at one time or another. Whether you've been friends since kindergarten or since

Thursday, you had to do the get-to-know-you dance, find common interests, build trust between you, and earn the memories through time spent together. Networking is like that. You're just back to the beginning of the process.

Back up for a second. I changed my mind. Asking my friends for connections was the second most emotionally vulnerable part of my personal networking challenge. Showing up in person was definitely the biggest, most daunting obstacle I faced.

In fact, I remember setting off to one of the very first in-person networking events to which I'd RSVP'd. All the way there, I practiced breathing. I went through my affirmations. I literally turned around and started for home before I pep-talked myself back onto the road. I wanted to throw up. In the end, I promised myself donuts from my very favorite, and very indulgent, local bakery—a treat that is normally reserved for the first and last days of school (and National Donut Day, of course).

In the end, I leapt, and the net did appear. I got out of the car, did more deep breathing, imagined how I wanted to show up, pulled out my business cards, and walked in with my head held high. I asked questions, I practiced some of the tips I'll share later in this book (such as sitting next to someone instead of sitting alone and offering compliments to my seatmates), and I networked the hell out of that luncheon.

Okay, maybe I wasn't that badass. In fact, if I'm being honest now, that whole luncheon was a blur of nerves and cold sweat.

The point is, I showed up. No matter how challenging and terrifying it was. I showed up.

When I was getting started on this networking journey (and still today), I used awareness, purpose, and intent to identify groups in which I knew I could connect with my ideal clients (women entrepreneurs and business owners). I joined a few women-only networking groups, a B2B networking group at my local chamber of commerce, and Toastmasters. My goal for each get-together was to find just one other woman with whom I could connect after the gathering for coffee, a phone call, or even a simple email follow-up.

Guess what. It sucked the first few (several...many...) times. But it eventually got less stressful. That muscle got stronger. I honed my strategies and found tricks that made it easier and more comfortable to connect with other attendees quickly.

Today, walking into events and new groups is easier. I won't lie, though. I still get nervous as hell.

But you know what's awesome about looking back to that very first in-person event I attended when I started this whole networking challenge? When I wanted to throw up on the ride over and had to bribe myself with donuts to get out of the car and enter the building? I met two women at that event who have become incredibly important in my life and my business. Before that terrifying day, I didn't know either of them from Bob. But today, they both sit on the Advisory Board of WEBO Network. One has become my accountability partner, without whom things like this book might not have ever happened; the other has taught me so much about manifesting the life I want.

These women are my tribe.

It boggles my mind to think that I wouldn't have met them if I hadn't taken the leap. Infinite possibilities, folks.

Infinite. Possibilities.

Prompts and Activities

- What mindjunk do you have that's keeping you from net-working successfully?

- How can you challenge that thinking and create a more positive story?

- What types of introductions would you like from family and friends (what's your purpose for asking)?

- To whom in your existing network of family and friends will you reach out?

GETTING REAL WITH YOUR GOALS

Earlier in this book, I mentioned I'd show you how creating awareness, purpose, and intent around your networking activities would give you a greater sense of control and take some of the emotional sting out of what can be an uncomfortable activity. In my work with business owners, I encourage them ignore the people "should-ing" all over them by getting clear about (awareness) their vision for themselves and their business (purpose), and then creating a clear plan for getting there (intent).

Have you ever done something you thought you should, only to feel as if it was one long slog? "Should" is an inherently shameful word, and when someone "shoulds" all over you—or worse, when you "should" all over yourself—you're bound to feel discord. The very definition of "should" is "to indicate obligation, duty, or correctness, typically when criticizing someone's actions." Obligation, duty...criticism. The very use of the word implies that you're not doing something you're supposed to, which fosters guilt, which reinforces negative self-talk, which goes hand in hand with self-reproach. Saying "I should network" means "I know that I and my business would benefit from networking." What's implied is "but I really don't want to" and "I feel guilty about it." Eesh.

One of the ways out of frustration is to connect emotionally with your goals for doing something. This creates awareness around your "why," and it's your why that inspires you and drives you to achieve the end goal. When you're aware of your why for networking, you can do it with purpose and intent. Instead of trying to answer someone else's should, you're defining your own intended result and directing your actions to reach it.

By owning your "why," and eliminating the discord of "should," you can say, "I'm going to network" (because you should and you are) or "I'm not going to network" (because you've made the choice not to and you're okay with that). When you're aware of your purpose for networking, you're empowered to make that choice. You can choose the groups, the people, and the desired outcome. That choice gives you a sense of connection and investment in the outcome of your activities. Everything seems easier, the next steps are clear, the process flows, and you're excited to tackle the obstacles and overcome them.

When you know why you're networking, you can choose the right groups and people to reach your goals.

Long story short, don't network because you "should." Network because you have goals and dreams and things you want to do in your business, and because you know that networking is the way to get there. Make the choice.

WHY WE NETWORK

Recently, a client and I had a conversation that went like this:

Client: I really enjoy networking with women and the relationships I build with them. But my ideal client is male. Should I be networking with men?

Me: (without a trace of irony) Only if you're networking to get more clients.

Okay, wait. Let me explain in case you're confused, because even I stumbled over that last bit there. The bit where I kinda-sorta said networking is about getting clients. Because I just spent several pages preaching that networking isn't sales. Because it isn't sales.

(Bear with me.)

We network for all sorts of reasons. Here are some of my favorites. We network to:

- Get a job
- Find an investor
- Establish partnerships
- Build a referral network
- Develop skills and knowledge
- Increase recognition for ourselves or our business, and (you betcha!)
- Get more clients for our business

What's *your* reason? Understanding your "why" in real, concrete terms (to find an investor, to grow your list, to get more clients) will help you evaluate if you're going about it in the most purposeful and effective ways.

Too many times I have clients say to me, "I've been networking my booty off and it's not helping my business. I'm not getting any results. Help!" Typically, these are the clients who fall victim to the "shoulds" and who are out there doing the thing with no plan or direction. For small businesses and entrepreneurs, networking can be one of the best ways to grow a business's reputation and revenue. That's why it's crucial that you develop goals and strategies for your networking activities.

Networking is a long game. I know I'm repeating myself, but a lot of people think networking is a quick fix. Show up at a meeting, pass around some cards, and—voila! New business. So. Not. True. Building relationships that pay off in supporting you and your business takes a lot of time (like, a lot), and any time you take away from your business is an investment, so I'll always caution you to spend time wisely. You wouldn't spend money in your business without a clear purpose and outcome in mind. Your time deserves to be treated with the same consideration.

YOUR NETWORKING GOALS

As a business owner, you know that you have to set goals in order to measure your progress. You set sales goals, hiring goals, performance goals, quality goals, budget goals...you can set goals for just about anything in your business. Add networking to that list.

Goal setting and creating strategies for achieving them is one of the main things I do with my clients. What I've learned is that, although we're taught to set huge, ginormous, pie-in-the-sky goals in life, we're rarely taught *how* to achieve them. We set grandiose goals without a clear timeline or path for how we'll get there. As soon as we reach a stumbling block or challenge, our goal falls apart because we didn't plan for obstacles. Before we know it, the goal evaporates. As Antoine de Saint-Exupéry said, "A goal without a plan is just a wish."

One of the best ways to create a plan for achieving your objectives in your business is to set SMART Goals. Setting SMART Goals helps you:

- Get clear on what you want to accomplish
- Focus your efforts
- Spend your resources wisely to get there, and
- Up the odds that you'll achieve what you set out to do

SMART is an acronym for Specific, Measurable, Actionable, Realistic, and Timebound. Big-picture goals can be overwhelming, but when you evaluate them based on these five criteria, create clear next steps, and then *work those steps,* you'll make consistent progress and eventually get to where you want to go.

S is for Specific

When it comes to networking, get specific with your goals. Like, super specific. It's not enough to say, "I want to grow my network." Technically, adding one name to your list is growing your network. But that's not really what you want, is it? Specific goals look like this: "I will increase my network by 25 percent before the end of the year, and at least half of those names will be qualified potential clients." Yowza! Now that's specific!

Specific doesn't necessarily have to mean huge or complicated. When I was putting myself through my personal networking challenge to overcome my fears, my goals were much simpler (albeit, still specific). My goal was to attend one networking group a week for three months and to come away with one one-on-one coffee date from each. Straightforward, simple, specific.

M is for Measurable

Whether your goal has a massive impact on your business, or results in small, incremental changes in your daily operations, being specific gives you parameters that you can measure against in order to evaluate the success of your efforts.

Let's face it. We humans like instant gratification, and sometimes it takes a while—a long while—to get to where we want to go in our business. We get bored. We get distracted (squirrel!). When we don't get an immediate reward, we tend to lose steam.

When you create specific goals that can be measured, you build in a system for keeping yourself motivated. Celebrating small milestones along the way to your end goal helps you keep your focus and excitement high.

More importantly, defining specific goals allows you to see if you're achieving what you set out to achieve. Think back to the clients who tell me they're shaking their networking booty and not getting any results. Frequently, when I start to dig deeper, I find out that they have, in fact, grown their list, built valuable partnerships, or been asked to speak to groups. So, they *are* getting results. The issue at hand is that they didn't have specifically defined goals for their efforts, so there's no way to determine if the results they're getting are the ones they wanted.

If you don't know where you want to go, you won't know when you've gotten there.

A is for Actionable

Or, how to get there. You can set specific, defined, measurable goals, but if you can't create the actions to get there, you're doomed. An actionable goal is a goal for which you have the resources, talents, and knowledge to "get 'er done."

For instance, if your goal is to grow your network by 25 percent before the end of the year, do you have access to the types of groups that will provide that number of new contacts? Do you have the time and the budget to join and attend those groups regularly? Do you have the resources to create solid lead follow-up systems? If you don't have them now, can you gain access to them in time to achieve your goal?

It may be that as you consider whether a goal is actionable and achievable for you, you realize that it requires resources and talents beyond your capacity. In that case, is the goal relevant to you and your business? If it is, then look at it as a growth opportunity—something to stretch your current capabilities and mindset. Maybe you want to add a new skill set, take a class, or invest in new technology in order to achieve your goal. Or, maybe you're ready to up your game by hiring help in an area where your skills are the weakest. In other words, actionable goals may not be actionable right now, but they can be a chance to expand your talents, your knowledge, or your business.

No single business goal exists in a vacuum. Any goal you set has to align with your overall business objectives.

R is for Realistic

Let's go back to the goal of increasing your network by 25 percent over the year. Can your business *realistically* support that increase in contacts? Can you serve the clients who are likely to result from that increase?

No single business goal exists in a vacuum. Any goal you set, whether it's networking, financial, marketing, or hiring, has to align with your overall business objectives. Everything we do in our business is interrelated and must both support and be supported by all our other business activities. Networking is no different. When we define our networking goals, they have to align with—and support—the other things we're doing in our business. Sometimes, those objectives require that we network for new clients. Sometimes, they mean we network for strategic partnerships, investors, or peer advisors. Understanding how your networking goals fit into your overall business plan is vital to creating the specific, measurable, actionable goals that will lead to your success.

T is for Timebound

When it comes to goal setting, naming a target date is key. Build the time frame into the goal itself (90 days, six months, one year...whatever works for you and your business) so that you have a constant sense of urgency. Why? Without a defined deadline, it's too easy to say "I'll get to that tomorrow" and then, well, you know. Building a time frame into your goal keeps everyday tasks from getting in the way of your ultimate objective, keeps you moving forward, and helps you achieve what you set out to achieve.

As with any business objectives, the key to achieving your networking targets is to make your goals relevant to you and your business, appropriate for the time and financial commitment you're willing and able to make, and (most importantly) attainable.

Whether you're networking for a job, an investor, a mentor, professional development, or (okay, fine) more clients, getting SMART about your networking goals can make you a SMARTer networker (Ha! See what I did there?).

Prompts and Activities

Need help setting your networking goals? Ask yourself:

- What is my primary business objective (remember, it may not be sales)? What's going on in my business right now that needs the most attention?

- How will networking support this objective? Whom do I need to meet to be successful?

- What do I want to accomplish (get specific—how much, how many)? How will I know when I've completed it?

- What steps will I take to achieve this goal? Can I break my overall goal into monthly, weekly, or daily tasks, or chunk it into sections that make sense to me?

- How will I measure progress along the way? Can I create milestone dates for each of the steps I outlined above?

- Do I have the resources (time, budget, support) to accomplish my goal? If not, how will I get them?

- What is my time frame for achieving this goal?

- How will I celebrate my success?

TIME AND MONEY, BABY

Now that you have a goal (a specific, measurable, actionable, realistic, timebound goal), it's time to start evaluating your networking options and creating a plan for your efforts. Like anything in business, it all comes down to time and money.

From here on out, we're going to get real about the time and money investment of networking. Networking includes hard costs (group fees, meals, cocktails) and soft costs (time). Good business owners track every dollar spent against every dollar made so that they can maximize their financial investments, eliminate money wasters, and make the most of their business budgets. Successful business owners also measure the return on investment (ROI) of their time for the same reasons.

Track your investment in networking like you would any business expense.

Simply put, ROI is a performance measure that evaluates the efficiency of an investment. Was the cost of that group/event, or the time you spent there, worth it to your business?

When you can measure your investments in ROI, you can see which activities are producing the best results. The formula for ROI is:

$$\frac{\text{(Gain from Investment - Cost of Investment)}}{\text{Cost of Investment}} = \text{ROI}$$

So, if you spent $625 to join a networking group, and you were able to track $2,500 in new business directly to your participation in that group, it would look like this:

$$\frac{(\$2,500 - \$625)}{\$625} = 300\%$$

You'd have an ROI of 300%. Woo-hoo!

On the other hand, if you attended a two-day conference that cost you $2,500 and you made a single connection that resulted in a strategic partnership that earned $10,000 worth of business, your ROI would also be 300%.

$$\frac{(\$10,000 - \$2,500)}{\$2,500} = 300\%$$

Measuring your ROI is an objective way of comparing your marketing and networking expenditures to see which are getting the greatest traction.

But what about time?

If you've been paying attention, there's a consistent, underlying theme to all this networking stuff. Time. While networking is one of the best ways for small businesses and entrepreneurs to increase their visibility, it's also time intensive. The most successful small businesses I know are those that dedicate significant amounts of time each week to engaging in networking activities. Being aware of this from the outset can save a lot of heartache.

Business owners who spent an average of six-plus hours a week networking generated almost 47 percent of their business through networking and referrals.

What if I told you that a recent study showed that people who spent an average of six-plus hours a week networking generated almost 47 percent of their business through networking and referrals?[6]

Six. Hours. A. Week.

How much time did you spend this week networking? I'm going to guess a lot less than six hours (if I'm wrong, then this probably isn't the book for you).

How much is your time worth?

Regardless of your industry, a small-business owner has a baseline hourly rate that they need to earn in order to sustain their business. If you don't know your hourly rate, it's okay. Many of my clients couldn't tell me theirs when we started to work together. But it's an important number, and I encourage you to take the time to find, understand, and set yours.

What's your hourly rate? Your hourly rate is the amount of money you need to make every hour that you work in order to cover your operating costs and desired salary. It's the threshold that determines whether you have a "jobby" (a hobby that makes some money) or a business.

Here's the dealio, business owner. If you're working and not covering your costs, then you're volunteering. If you're covering costs, but not making a profit, then you're running a not-for-profit business (literally). Businesses exist to make money and bring profits to their owners. Understanding what it takes to do that is a fundamental part of owning and succeeding at your own business.

But, I digress.

To calculate your hourly rate, add your desired annual salary to all the expenses of running your business (internet, software, paper, printer ink, subscriptions, coaching fees, coffee—literally anything you spend money on in your business or office). Include healthcare and taxes. The resulting amount is your adjusted annual salary.

What does that look like? Here's a quick example:

Your desired annual salary	$75,000
Your monthly operating costs x 12 months	$12,000
Healthcare (annual)	$4,800
Self-employment tax (annual)	$5,700
Add those up to get your new adjusted annual salary...	**$97,500**

Now, how many hours are you going to work each year? There are 2,080 working hours in a year (52 weeks x 40 hours). Factor in the number of sick days, vacation days, and holidays you want to take to determine your hours off. For example:

Sick days: 5 days x 8 hours..40 hours

Vacation: 3 weeks x 40 hours .... 120 hours

Holidays: 7 days x 8 hours ....56 hours

Total hours off for the year..216 hours

2,080 hours – 216 hours................ **1,864 working hours per year**

Except, you won't really be working 1,864 hours a year. That number assumes that you're working 40 hours per week and that every hour you're working, you're performing client work (aka making money). As a business owner, you know that you also need time to work on phone calls, administrative tasks, networking, and other back-office duties. We need to account for those hours, so let's assume those nonbillable tasks take up 25 percent of your time:

$$1,864 \times 75\% = 1,398 \text{ Annual Billable Hours}^*$$

This assumes a 40-hour work week; you'll need adjust calculations if you're aiming for a less-than-full-time business.

Phew. Almost there. Once you know how many billable hours you expect to work in a year, you can easily calculate your necessary hourly rate (necessary because it ensures that you'll cover your business expenses *and* achieve your salary goals). To calculate your hourly rate, divide your adjusted annual salary by your annual billable hours:

$$\frac{\$97,500}{1,398 \text{ HRS}} = \$69.75 \text{ Hourly Rate}$$

If you work 40 hours a week (less your vacation, holidays, and sick time) all year, you need to earn $69.75 each and every hour to sustain your business and pay yourself your desired salary. That's what your time is worth.

Now...where were we? Oh, yes. ROI on time.

Once you know your hourly rate, you can calculate the ROI of the time you're spending on networking activities.

CALCULATING THE ROI OF NETWORKING

Let's use the first example from earlier, but compare the return on your time. In this example, you joined a networking group for $625 and gained $2,500 in new business from the relationships within the group. Since we're measuring time and not money in this case, we'll assume that that new business was realized after six months of group participation. We'll also assume the group met for one hour each week, was local, and required 20 minutes of travel time each way to meetings. If the group meets weekly, that means you spent 24 hours in the group and 16 hours on the road, for a total of 40 hours. In the same six-month period, you also spent an additional 12 hours engaging in one-on-one coffees with each of the members in the group, which brings your time investment up to 52 hours.

$$52 \text{ HOURS} \times \$69.75 = \$3,627 \text{ TIME COST}$$

52 hours of your time is worth $3,627 based on your hourly rate of $69.75.

Remember that the formula for ROI is:

$$\frac{\text{(Gain from Investment - Cost of Investment)}}{\text{Cost of Investment}} = \text{ROI}$$

So in our example measuring time:

$$\frac{(\$2,500 - \$3,627)}{\$3,627} = -31\%$$

Participating in this group cost you $3,627 in your time. Therefore, the ROI was −31%.

Not so great.

When we look at the second example, things look a little different. The two-day conference was 16 hours long, and you spent two hours traveling each way, plus two hours networking after the conference closed each day. After the conference, you spent an additional six hours on phone calls and emails with your new partner, setting up the details of your agreement. In total, you spent 30 hours of your time to secure the partnership that brought in a $10,000 contract. Thus, your time cost was $2,092.50,

$$30 \text{ HOURS} \times \$69.75 = \$2,092.50 \text{ TIME COST}$$

and the ROI of your attendance at the conference was 377%.

$$\frac{(\$10,000 - \$2,092.50)}{\$2,092.50} = 377\%$$

No, I'm not saying ditch your networking groups and spend all your time at conferences. What I *am* saying is that by creating specific, measurable goals and tracking your results, you can get a clear picture of which of your networking efforts are, literally, paying off. The apples-to-apples comparison of the financial investment in the two scenarios was identical; however, the time comparison was vastly different. (Note: always compare apples to apples, never apples to oranges, or apples to carrots.) In other words, if your pain point is financial, you may want to focus on the money you're investing in your networking. If, like me, time is your enemy, then use your hourly rate and hours spent as your measure.

As with everything else in this book, I'm going to tell you that how you invest in networking—with both your finances and your time—is entirely dependent on you, your goals, and your business. There's no right or wrong answer. There's only the right answer for you (but, damn, that six-plus hours a week number is quite compelling).

I've just shown you two ways to measure ROI based on investments of money and time. Either one works. Or, you can combine your hard costs (money) with the soft costs (hourly rate), run the same calculations, and come up with a third percentage. Whatever measure you use has to make sense for you and your business. Which is more important to you, your money or your time? Which do you guard more closely? Which do you have more of?

Many corporations allocate 1 to 3 percent of an employee's salary for professional development activities like networking.

The trickiest part of the whole game is *setting* those budgets for money and time. One of the most frequent questions I get is, "How much should I spend on networking?" Again, no right answer here (sorry!). If it helps, many corporations set aside about 1 to 3 percent of an employee's annual salary for professional development.[7] What would 1 to 3 percent of your gross revenue amount to for networking and training?

Regardless of your budget, creating awareness about how much you're willing and able to invest in your networking will help you set realistic expectations on the results, and it will eliminate some of the "I've been networking my booty off with no results" angst. When you know how much you can invest, you can be purposeful about the groups you join and the amount of time you spend each week in those groups. You can design a plan that will help you achieve your goals and get you the traction you want.

Prompts and Activities

When determining how much money and time you have to spend on networking (or anything), ask yourself:

- How much time do I realistically have available to spend networking each week (after allowing time for client work, marketing, and administrative tasks, as well as travel time to and from my engagements)?

- How much money do I have available to me to invest in networking groups and activities? (This is a good place to stretch yourself slightly, as the most expensive groups are frequently the best. More on that in the next chapter.)

Sounds simple enough, right? Show of hands: How many of you have ever asked yourself these questions? Yep. I thought so. Stick around. By the end of this book, we'll incorporate the answer to these questions (and others) to create a solid networking plan (and budget) for you and your business.

FINDING THE RIGHT GROUP FOR YOUR NETWORKING STYLE

I'm going to let you in on a little secret. Whether you know it or not, you're already a champ at networking. Go you!

Don't believe me? Remember our friend Bob (RIP) and the tribe that left him behind? The pre-people who formed relationships, stuck together, and escaped the lions passed down the genetic drivers that *instinctually* help us build interpersonal connections for survival.

That same urge to connect socially is what makes you a successful networker without even trying. In fact, one of the definitions of networking is "the exchange of information among individuals, groups, or institutions."

Every time someone asks you, "What do you do?" and you answer, you're networking.

You exchange information with other humans all the time, and in doing so, you're consciously or unconsciously (instinctually) cultivating those key relationships. Every time someone asks you "What do you do?" and you answer, you're networking.

Kids' soccer game? Networking!

Book club? Networking!

Waiting in line at the DMV? Networking!

Chatting up your hair stylist? Networking!

Popping onto social media? Networking!

We do it for our emotional and mental health.

We do it to get the resources we need.

We do it because it makes us happy.

We do it so that we don't end up like Bob.

We're hardwired to connect with people, and we do. All day, every day in a hundred—actually, a thousand—different ways.

Well, then (I'm imagining your voice in my head), if I'm so great at it already, why do I need your book to tell me how to do it?

Great question! I just said that you're networking consciously or unconsciously all the time. I want to eliminate the "unconsciously" from your activities and make you a networking dynamo by creating awareness around what you're doing so that you can be purposeful and intentional in your efforts. It's that awareness, purpose, and intent that will get you the results you're after.

Sure, when you're at your kids' soccer game and someone asks you what you do for a living, you can absolutely chat them up, share your business, and (potentially) get some traction out of the conversation. But that's not being very purposeful or intentional in cultivating a productive relationship for business. After all, you're not there for the business connections. You're there to watch little Bobby score.

Having the same conversation in a leads group or mastermind meeting can have an entirely different outcome. Because you're aware of your purpose for being there, and the other attendees are equally aware of their purpose, and because the intent of the meeting is clear, the conversations that arise and the connections that are made are deliberate and more likely to foster a mutually beneficial business relationship. Boom!

Putting yourself in the right places to make those purposeful connections is key. Taking the time to define your goals for networking (Chapter 3—done!), and allocating the right resources (Chapter 4—done!) will help you find the right networking channels to achieve your objectives.

A quick note about money and time and the weird correlation between them and the quality of a networking channel or group. You might imagine that your best investment of time and money would be in free groups that have the highest number of people. After all, if networking were sales, you'd want to reach the most people possible in the shortest amount of time with the least amount of expense.

But (say it with me) *networking isn't sales,* and it doesn't play by the same rules. Typically, the more expensive a group, the fewer people it has. But the quality of the relationships you build are higher, and the results for your business over time are better. Conversely, the least expensive (or free) events and groups with the most people don't always lead to the same number of high-quality connections.

Likewise, the most expensive groups, with the highest quality connections, frequently require a much greater time commitment—and I do mean commitment (see the discussion under Leads Groups below)—while free groups sometimes seem as though they couldn't care less if you come or if you go.

In other words, the highest quality connections usually require a little more skin in the game. Which is neither good nor bad, and both types of groups have their pros and cons. But it's something to be aware of as you start to evaluate groups against your goals and resources.

Let's start with some of the more common networking channels and group types.

ONLINE NETWORKING

For the networking-averse, online networking is a godsend. No face-to-face meeting means even the most socially awkward among us are capable of building vast virtual networks. Plus, it's fast, free, and easy.

But the fast, free, easy nature of online networking is also its downside. Because connections are formed and maintained virtually, the "ties that bind" are not as strong as in-person relationships. In order to be successful online, you have to stay active—like, all the time. Profiles on your social network accounts need to be updated continually, and you have to be proactive about regularly connecting with new people. Plan to spend time every day engaging with your existing network and adding new contacts.

Pros

Online platforms such as LinkedIn, Facebook, and Twitter allow you to build beautiful pages for yourself or your business. You can create custom headers, include your logos, and write eloquent descriptions of who you are and what you do. Most platforms also provide easy links and buttons that let your clients and potential clients connect and interact with you directly through messaging or emails. All of this is great for building your brand and visibility.

The magic of the interwebs also allows you to join special interest groups and use hashtags to deliver messages right to your ideal client. Niche sites targeted to your industry give you the opportunity to ask questions and build professional partner networks. Basically, online networking allows you to find your people, regardless of where they are, cheaply and easily.

Cons

Because of the impersonal nature of online networking, it can be hard to move those relationships off-line to create real connections. So, while it can be a great tool for spreading your brand, it can be more difficult to create the interpersonal relationships successful networking thrives on.

Unfortunately, many people who rely heavily on online networking don't seem to have gotten the memo that *networking isn't sales.* I'm sure I'm not the only person to have accepted a flattering LinkedIn request—for example, "As an industry leader, I'd like to connect with you on LinkedIn" (aw, shucks)—only to be bombarded with sales and promotional messages. The I-wouldn't-know-you-if-I-ran-into-you-and-you-were-wearing-a-name-tag quality of online networking makes it easier to cross that line with little or no hesitation.

NETWORKING EVENTS

A time-honored tradition, these large (and largely anony-mous) events are what we all think of when we think of network-ing. These events give me the heebie-jeebies. They usually take place in large space because they attract large crowds (big room). The networking is kind of a free-for-all. You check in, get your name tag, and wade into the crowd, hoping to make connections but mostly battling social anxiety and uncertainty (scary). My mindjunk story around these types of events goes something like this: "They all know each other already—look how they're laugh-ing and talking together. Oooh, that guy just gave me side-eye. She just whispered to her friend about me. No one is approaching me to introduce themselves" (not-friendly strangers). So, that's it. Big room. Scary. Not-friendly strangers.

In other words, lots and lots of lions.

These types of events are a hard nut to crack. Everyone is there to promote themselves and to pass out as many of their own business cards in as short amount of time as possible. The relationship-building opportunities presented by this traditional networking are fairly low. It's conceivable (but not likely) that you might bump up against someone who's looking for the exact ser-vice you offer at exactly the time they need it. The prospect that your business card is going to stand out from the handfuls that attendees will take home is also pretty slim.

Which is not to say that you shouldn't attend this type of event. It's always good to meet with people and build connections. Find events marketed to your ideal customer and others in your pro-fession. This allows you to get your message in front of the people who are most likely to buy your product and service, and it gives you the opportunity to create professional relationships.

Pros

There's an event like this every day and night of the week. Do a quick Google search, scroll through the calendars of your local chambers of commerce, or browse Meetup.com, and you're bound to find a multitude of after-hour events, speaking programs, lunches, or ribbon cuttings going on right now.

Cons

Overwhelm. There can literally be hundreds of people at these events, depending on the host, location, and time of day. And if there's free food? Fuhgeddaboutit! As I mentioned earlier, the chances that you'll push up against someone, strike up a conversation, and have it be a mutually beneficial (goals! resources!) connection are slim. You can increase your odds of success by being selective and targeted in the events you attend, but it's still kind of a crapshoot.

You can make these "cattle call" type events more successful by having a plan, which we'll talk more about in Chapter 10.

LEADS GROUPS

I have a love-hate relationship with leads groups. These are relationship-based organizations where the expectation is that members will provide business leads to each other. The benefit of this is that other members of the group are helping to pimp out your business, but (on the flip side), you're committed to driving clients and contacts to them as well as your own business. And I do mean "committed," because many leads groups have a baseline amount of business you're required to bring to other members of the group.

Leads groups are frequently sponsored by local chambers of commerce or by private, for-profit organizations such as BNI.com.

Pros

Typically noncompetitive, leads groups allow only one representative from any business category as a member at any given time. This eliminates competition and allows members to direct all business to the one roofer/banker/dog groomer in the group.

Regular group meetings and an established membership mean that these groups offer more robust relationship-building than networking events or online networking. And many times members form strong relationships and partnerships outside the group meetings. The primary purpose of a leads group is generating referrals, so these are a good option for an entrepreneur looking for allies to actively promote their business.

Cons

Because their purpose is to foster strong relationships, leads groups commonly meet weekly and have strict attendance guidelines. As mentioned earlier, some organizations also closely track the leads generated in the group, and you're expected to achieve a certain dollar amount in leads for your fellow members. If a weekly commitment doesn't fit your schedule, or the added pressure of promoting other businesses doesn't work with your personality or your own business objective, a leads group might not be the right networking avenue for you.

Leads groups may not be a good fit for internet-based business-es, nontraditional businesses, or super-nichey businesses. These types of groups are best for traditional, local businesses (pest control, banking, real estate) that operate within a defined geographic area. The less mainstream your business is, the harder it will be for other members in the group to bring you leads or referrals.

MASTERMIND GROUPS OR PEER ADVISORY BOARDS

Although not generally considered true networking, master-mind groups and peer advisory boards foster strong relationships between members on a business and personal level. Typically, each member is invited to share their professional and private challenges and successes, during which a business coach and other members of the group offer support and encouragement in finding solutions as well as celebrate accomplishments. This willingness to be vulnerable can lead to strong connections between members that frequently develop into joint venture opportunities, lead sharing, and professional networking.

Mastermind groups and peer advisory boards are often built around a common member trait, whether its length of time in business, revenue amount, industry type, or some other characteristic that is shared among participants.

Pros

Mastermind groups offer a combination of brainstorming, education, peer accountability, and support in a group setting, which offers professional development along with the opportunity to build deep interpersonal connections with other members. Many masterminds are noncompetitive, and members are encouraged to dig deep in sharing and offering advice to each other on the most intimate parts of their business. The peer-to-peer mentoring and professional coaching of a combined group coaching and mastermind provide a profound opportunity for an entrepreneur to maximize their networking efforts from a personal, professional, and business-growth standpoint. (Note: I'm a huge fan of masterminding! WEBO Network started with a couple of mastermind groups, and those programs remain a key component of the organization.)

Cons

Because masterminds are typically offered in a small-group format, they can be hard to find, hard to join, and expensive. Many professional masterminding organizations have a high buy-in, and you have to be earning in the mid- to high six figures to be eligible to join their entry-level groups. You can Google business masterminds or peer advisory boards in your area, but one of the best ways to find one is to start asking your business network with whom and where they're masterminding. Or you can start your own!

EDUCATIONAL NETWORKING GROUPS

Like masterminds and peer advisory groups, educational networking groups offer more than just a chance to connect. Groups like WEBO Network and 3to5 Clubs offer professional development and experiential learning opportunities that help you improve your business sense and grow your skills as a business owner while you build mutually beneficial relationships with other members.

These groups can be industry-related or cover a general scope, such as women in business, start-ups, or B2B.

Pros

I built WEBO network based on my personal networking style. Because educational groups typically provide a program or speaker as the focus of their events, it can take the social pressure off of connecting with other members whom you may not know. Learning and interacting side by side as you engage in an activity or enjoy a presentation can be much less intimidating than the typical handshake-and-what-do-you-do-may-I-have-your-card interaction of a meet-and-greet type of networking event because it provides you with an opportunity to ask questions and offer natural input on the discussion.

Cons

On the flip side, because the focus of these events is not necessarily on mingling or networking, you do need to be aware and purposeful about making connections. We'll talk more about how to identify the right people to ask for further engagement, but participating in the conversation and staying tuned in to what others are contributing can help you pick out your coffee-date targets.

PROFESSIONAL ASSOCIATIONS

These associations exist for professional development through the exchange of information and ideas, and they're designed for people from one specific type of industry, such as design, engineering, finance, or health. Ask your best (most ideal) customers which groups they belong to.

Pros

If your ideal customer or partner falls into a single industry, these groups and their events can be fertile ground for your networking efforts. Attending events and programs targeted at your ideal client will also help inform your messaging, as it gives you an opportunity to learn more about their industry-specific concerns and pain points.

Cons

While some groups allow businesses from outside the industry to join as affiliates or associates, many professional associations don't allow vendors to join as full members. If you find this to be the case, consider ways that you can be of value to the group without being "salesy." Can you sponsor the printing of some of their materials? Volunteer to run their social media? Donate space for their events?

These groups are also good targets for offering programs or presentations that offer value as well as useful information to members. They position you as an expert in your industry without an overt selling approach.

When it comes to finding and joining networking events, leads groups, professional associations, or educational networking groups, the interwebs is definitely your best friend. Play around with search terms that include your industry or special interests. Check out your local chamber of commerce, as it most likely offers at least a couple—if not all—of these types of groups on its calendar.

And be sure to hit up your existing network of friends and colleagues to get input on the groups that have worked for them—especially the more elusive mastermind and peer advisory groups. Remember, just as their business is different from yours, their networking goals may be different too. Drill down in your questions to ask them why they like the groups they like, what they've gotten out of them, and whether they'd suggest membership for someone with your unique objectives.

Humans tend to operate on instinct. It's our default setting. But instinct isn't always the best place to settle if you want something more out of life than survival.

Being conscious of your personal networking style and what you want to achieve through your networking will help you find the groups that not only feel comfortable but that will enable you to build the *right* connections for reaching your goals.

Prompts and Activities

- Based on your current goals and objectives, what types of organizations and groups would be the right fit for your networking activities?

- Ask your top clients where they're networking with others in their industry. Connect with colleagues you admire to ask where they've had success networking.

DO YOUR RESEARCH

Remember *Goldilocks and the Three Bears*? The story goes something like this: The Bear family leaves home for a trip to the mall and forgets to set the home alarm. (What? It's the twenty-first century, let's modernize this little tale!) For reasons no one has ever been able to explain to me, Mama Bear decides to make their porridge just before they all hop into the bear-mobile, and they leave the porridge to cool on the table while they head off to do a little shopping. Along comes Goldilocks, who smells the delicious porridge through the window and lets herself into the house. (Um, hello? Neighborhood Watch?)

Before her on the table are three bowls of porridge. First, Goldilocks tries Daddy Bear's porridge, which is too hot. Then, she tries Mama Bear's porridge, which is too cold. Finally, she tries Baby Bear's porridge, and it's (say it with me) JUST RIGHT!

Long story short, Goldie goes through this same trial and error with some chairs (too big, too small, JUST RIGHT!) and some beds (too hard, too soft, JUST RIGHT!), and probably some other stuff because the girl has boundary issues.

We all know how that story ended. And, no, I don't for a second believe that the bears were all like, "Gee, who's been eating my porridge?" Bears aren't super forgiving. And, they're pretty territorial. I always thought my mom was sugar-coating it when she said that Goldilocks made it out alive.

But, Goldie had the right idea.

You have to try things on for size to see if they're JUST RIGHT. Especially in business.

Show of hands: when's the last time you bought something for your business without doing research? Have you ever bought a computer without comparing features and prices? Or hired a consultant without meeting them first or checking out their references? No, you're way too smart for that.

Which is why when you choose networking groups and events, I want you to do your due diligence and research before you commit any resources (Time! Money!).

Whether you're looking at a networking event or a mastermind group or a civic organization like the Rotary Club, every organization—and every chapter of an organization—has a different personality. That personality varies based on the mission and purpose of the organization. This includes the make-up of the chapter (both the member personalities and the businesses represented), the agenda and structure of the meetings, the location of the meetings, the frequency of the meetings, the leadership of the group, and a million other tangible and intangible factors. It's up to you as a potential member and investor in that organization to figure out if the personality of the group is a good fit for you. After all, if you're going to commit time and money to participating, not only do you want the group to make sense for your business, but (ideally) you want to enjoy your time there.

Let me rephrase that. You *definitely* want to enjoy your time in a group. You want to have fun, and you want to be able to like the other members. Networking is about building those connections and mutually beneficial relationships. It's hard to connect with people when you're unhappy, and it's damn near impossible to connect with people when you don't like and respect them. Because (ahem!) we do business with people we know, like, and trust.

We've all been to networking groups and events where we just didn't feel a connection, haven't we? How many of us have then gone on to join that group but never really shook that feeling of "meh" we had the first time? I know I have.

When I was researching groups for my own business networking activities, I asked around to see where my associates were networking. The name of one group came up a few times from several different contacts, so I thought I'd try it out. On paper, it looked like the perfect fit. It met once a month, which suited my time requirements; it fell well within my financial budget; and it was a women-only group. I did what I thought was pretty thorough due diligence. I read the group's website, asked questions of the members I knew, did a little LinkedIn recon to see what the group discussions were about, and visited a meeting.

My first impressions were good. The caliber of the women in the room was impressive. They seemed to genuinely like each other, and I could tell that they were connecting outside the meeting times. So far, the group was checking all my boxes.

But.

The meeting was heavily structured, and there wasn't much time for conversation or connection during the meeting itself—which means I was choosing who I wanted to connect with individually on the basis of their elevator speeches. There was also a lot of "group business" on the agenda, with limited time for introductions by group members. The meeting included a speaker presentation, but the topic wasn't totally relevant to business. It had more of a personal- development slant (as opposed to professional development). None of these were deal breakers, but they did register as concerns.

I liked my first meeting...enough.

I joined.

And that feeling of "meh" never quite went away.

Which is odd because I actually made some great connections during my time in the group. I've collaborated with other members and found great professional development opportunities. I've been able to tap into the brain power of some amazing business owners. A couple of the women and I have partnered on projects and bartered services. Several members of that group also joined WEBO Network, so I was able to interact with them in even more settings.

Unfortunately, I never got around to truly enjoying the meetings, and I usually spent my time there checking the Book of Faces on my phone. And then I started to skip the monthly meetings because they weren't really fun for me. Which is a shame because I did invest quite a bit of time—and no little bit of money—in belonging to that group. In the end, I decided that, on balance, it had been a valuable experience. I'd added some worthwhile connections to my network, and I'd learned what to look for in a networking experience.

Listen, there were and are women who love that group. They're evangelists, they sing its praises, and they've drunk the Kool Aid. Which is fine. Because it aligns with their goals and their objectives. They're getting what they need out of it and they enjoy being part of it. They have fun.

Again, I want you to have fun networking. When you're having fun, you're more relaxed. When you're more relaxed, you're more authentic. It's that authenticity that will help you connect with other people in a meaningful way.

But I also want you to be real about what's serving you and your business. You can definitely have fun *and* keep your eye on your professional objectives at the same time. It's totally doable. In short, I'm encouraging you to recognize what you like best about networking groups and to find the right type of group with the right personality for you.

MAKE A VISIT

First, and most important, visit every group you might conceivably consider joining. Yes, this sucks up a lot of time, but there's no way to understand the feel and personality of a group or chapter until you've sat there and experienced it for yourself. When I'm on the hunt for new groups to add to my schedule, I try to hit one new organization a week (psst...that's a Specific goal). Sometimes, it works out that I have to do more than one per week and none during other weeks, based on the meeting calendars of different groups. But because I'm aware of my schedule and business demands, I can identify when that's doable and when I might have to wait until the following month to make a visit to a group I'm interested in.

When I pop into a new group to see if it's JUST RIGHT for me and my business, I'm looking for a couple of things. First, who's there and how they're interacting. After all, I'm there to meet the people—I want to make sure the people in the room are the ones I want to meet. Second, I pay close attention to the chairs. Seriously. How a room is set up is key to the interactions that take place before, during, and after a meeting. Third, I'm super-aware of how the meeting flows. I know I want a meeting with ample opportunity for members to connect. I want activities and opportunities within the agenda to facilitate those connections. And I want the information shared to be relevant to me and my goals. Last, and most important, I'm tuned in to how many attendees are scheduling follow-up meetings with each other. Do people stay and mingle—phones out, calendars open—after the formal meeting wraps up?

Some organizations, including WEBO Network, offer a calendar of different types of events. For instance, we have a monthly luncheon, a monthly professional development event, and a monthly after-hours, in addition to our mastermind programs and special groups. Each type of event has a different feel, agenda, and audience, based on member interests. If the organizations you're considering offer multiple platforms, visit as many as you can to see which appeal to you the most before deciding whether to join the group.

EVALUATE HOW YOU FEEL

Those are the group attributes that are JUST RIGHT for me. But remember, there's no right or wrong answer to which group is JUST RIGHT for you. It all depends on you and your business objectives. Once you're aware of your networking goals and the types of groups that can support them, the next step is to build your awareness of how you want your networking experience to *feel*.

If you're new at this networking thing, or if you've been out there shaking your booty with no results, it may be that you aren't quite sure of what you're looking for in a networking group. Think about your learning style, your comfort level in introducing yourself to strangers, and what makes you feel most comfortable in a group. Once you get some clarity about the types of networking situations in which you feel most comfortable, go out and visit some groups and see if they check your boxes.

- **When you're visiting a group, pay attention to how other members interact.** Do they seem comfortable with each other? Are they chatting about events and things they've done together outside the meeting? Is there time to mingle before and after the structured part of the meeting? Are people approaching you, or are they standoffish? Are you being included in the casual conversations taking place before and after the meeting? Are you part of the tribe, or are you being left to the lions?

- **Take a look around at how the room is set up.** Some groups sit around one big conference-style table, which means everyone can see and hear everyone else. At networking events over meals, they might have you separated into tables of eight to ten people. Educational groups sometimes use rows of seats, similar to what you might find in a classroom or lecture hall. None of these is right or wrong, good or bad. But by paying attention to the physical arrangement of the room, you can gauge how freely people are able to interact before, during, and after the structured portion of the meeting.

- **During the meeting itself, pay attention to the flow of the agenda.** How much time do people have to formally introduce themselves to the group? What is the demeanor of members while they're introducing themselves. Are they laughing, smiling, and sharing jokes as they give their elevator speech? Or, are they stiff and formal and adhering to a script? How does the hostess or leader conduct the meeting? Is there time for open discussion, or does the meeting stick to a strict agenda? What types of topics are covered? Is there a directed discussion or table topic that allows everyone to participate in a conversation, or is the talking limited to the hostess/leader?

- **Finally, and maybe most importantly, how do you feel when you're in the room?** What's your first impression of the group? Do you feel welcomed? Are you interested in the conversations and meeting topics? Are you bored? Are the people in the room friendly and open? Are they engaging in a way that's comfortable for you?

Are you excited to come back?

Remember, your goal is to find groups in which you feel comfortable and able to genuinely connect with other members. Your purpose for participating in a networking group is to build mutually beneficial relationships. The groups that are JUST RIGHT for you will let you be yourself, relax, have fun, and connect with other members in a real way that will benefit you and your business objectives.

Prompts and Activities

When evaluating what you want from a networking group, ask yourself questions such as:

- Do I like a lot of structure, or do I prefer to be left on my own to connect?

- Do I like to engage in activities, or do I prefer people to make presentations to me?

- Do I like to dress up for business events, or do I prefer events at which I can show up in my normal, everyday attire?

- Do I prefer to be included in a conversation or lesson, or do I prefer to hang back and not contribute?

- Do I feel more comfortable in a formal, professional setting or in a casual, less stuffy environment?

- Do I feel comfortable raising my hand to contribute to a conversation, or do I prefer to be asked for my input?

- Am I comfortable mingling in a large group, or do I prefer being organized into small groups or tables to make connections?

- Am I comfortable eating in front of strangers (seriously, this is something to consider), or would I prefer an event without food?

- Which past experiences in networking groups have been positive and which have been negative? Why?

THE FIVE CS

In the last chapter, we talked about the different types of networking events and how you can evaluate whether they're the right place to spend your time and money. Once you've picked the one(s) that is JUST RIGHT for you and your business, the next step is assessing the *members* of the group to determine who is going to be JUST RIGHT to engage with outside of the group meeting or event.

My personal networking challenge has morphed into a kind of field study of networking habits. Maybe I should give it a formal title? Something like "Misinterpretations of the Mechanics and Techniques for Constructing Interpersonal Relationships and Professional Networks Among North American Entrepreneurs and Small-Business Owners: A Field Study." Oooh, very fancy!

Okay, we'll leave the title alone for now.

Since beginning my personal networking challenge, I've been paying more and more attention to how people network. Or try to network. Because I've noticed something. They're going about it all willy-nilly.

I'm going to stop here for a second. Show of hands: How many of you make a one-on-one date with someone at every single networking event? Mmmm-hmmm...

Remember my bootyless clients who are out there networking with no results? "I'm doing all the things!" they say. "I'm going to all the groups! I'm passing out cards! I'm meeting the people! But I'm just not getting any traction!" When I start asking questions, one of the main facts I find is that they are, indeed, doing all the things. Meetings, cards, handshakes—the whole shebang. What they're not doing is taking those connections beyond that meeting to having one-on-ones with them. Or, if they are, they're not choosing the right people to connect with.

Listen. To. Me. It isn't enough to attend a group meeting, share your elevator speech, spend 10 minutes schmoozing other attendees, and then go home and wait for the phone to ring. Remember our discussion about relationships and how much time it takes to build a solid one? How much time you invested in your connections before they shifted from "acquaintance" to "friend"? From "date" to "boyfriend" to "husband"?

These deeper connections are formed when we spend time with people. When we go beyond the 30- to 60-second introduction to find mutual interests, share pictures of our dogs, or discover we grew up three streets from each other. Sure, the business talk is one piece, but the know, like, and trust part is the nut of the relationship. By engaging with people one on one, with no distractions, we're able to find common ground, foster regard for each other, and build rapport. *Then* we get into the zone of possibility!

When I go to a networking meeting, I know before I enter the room how many one-on-one connections I want to come away with. I've looked at my schedule, and I know what I'm doing in my business, what my immediate and long-term goals are, and what types of connections I need to make them happen. So, I find the people at that event that fit the bill. Then, I ask them for a one-on-one.

I'm going to let you in on a little secret. Sometimes I *don't* make dates with people. Sometimes I'm just tired, running on low energy, or in the midst of a huge project with no daylight in my schedule. But I always, always, have a plan when I attend an event. So, even if the plan is not to organize any one-on-ones that day, it's still a plan.

Now that you (I hope) see the importance of connecting with the people you meet beyond the group event, let's talk about who you're connecting with.

First, let's review. In order to make networking succeed for you, you need to be aware of your:

- Overall business goals and objectives
- Resources (Time! Money!)

And when you know those things, you can be purposeful about the:

- Groups you join
- People you connect with

As with many things in business, to network effectively, you have to be laser-focused on what you want to achieve and how you're going to achieve it. You chose your groups based on the organization's membership and mission. Now that you're in the group, take it one step further and identify those members who are most likely to help you reach your goals and objectives.

Remember, we network for many different reasons. We network to find jobs, to find investors, to find partners, to grow our own knowledge and skills, to find resources for our own business, to find clients, and a million other reasons. Although choosing the right group helps you narrow down the types of people you'll most likely come into contact with, you still need to be aware of who's in the room with you and who you want to connect with further.

Recently, a client and I were discussing how I approach people for one-on-ones in a group setting. I was explaining my tactics (which I'll also explain to you in a later section) when she asked, "What about someone who's across the room who I didn't have a chance to talk to during the meeting?"

I asked her why she wanted to connect with that person, and she shrugged and said, "I don't know, it's just someone I hadn't met before..."

So. Yeah. Willy-nilly.

Listen, I don't know about you, but I'd much rather have lunch with my besties than put on the business face and spend time with complete strangers. After all, my friends are my tribe. Strangers? Might as well be lunching with lions.

I mean, seriously? Networking is exhausting. You have to be "on." All. The. Time. You have to repeat your spiel again and again, and ask the same questions again and again. Your social brain is on overload. I never feel completely relaxed or that I can let my guard down when I'm doing a one-to-one with someone new. After all, I'm trying to get them to know, like, and trust me! But with my squad? They already know me (warts and all), I'm pretty sure they like me most of time, and they seem to trust me (I have their garage codes). So, yeah, I'd much rather spend my time with them.

Which is why I'm purposeful about who I connect with one on one. I want to know that the time I'm spending in getting to know someone is spent getting to know the right someone for my goals and objectives.

I'm going to share what I call the Five Cs: Connectors, Collaborators, Contractors, Clients, and Cool Kids. This is how I categorize the people I meet at networking events, and how I decide whether they're people I need to meet with individually now, later—or never.

CONNECTORS

Connectors are people who know the people you want to know, usually potential clients. For instance, if you're a Christian women's life coach, an ideal connector for you would be a pastor, a pastor's wife, or someone involved in a church's programming. If you're a health and wellness coach, your connector might be a chiropractor or physical therapist.

Connectors are plugged into specific communities and have a wide network of their own that fits the profile of people you want to get to know. They're the type of people who can help you reach your target audience easily.

There are also people I call "Master Connectors." They have an extraordinary ability to make friends and acquaintances (like you, when you finish this book!). Typically very open and friendly, these are people who genuinely like other people. We all know people like this. They're the ones who always offer to introduce you to so-and-so, or have a lawyer/accountant/dog washer they could recommend, or wonder if you know *name drop* because that person wrote a book/has a podcast/is speaking at an event you might like. These people aren't snooty about their connections. In fact, they're incredibly generous about sharing, and they're always on the lookout for ways to offer value and hook you up with someone who could help you reach your objectives.

Networking with connectors is easy because they love it. But connectors carry the risk when they introduce you to their contacts. So, be ready to earn their trust. Show up. Show interest in them. Offer value without asking for anything in return. Be consistent and deliberate in your interactions with them. Let them offer to make introductions; don't be pushy about getting to their people. In other words, be someone they'd be proud to introduce to their network.

COLLABORATORS

Collaborators are your strategic partners, with whom you can team up to offer more and better services to your clients. Usually, your collaborators have a noncompetitive business, but a similar client profile. For example, a copywriter teaming with a graphic designer or a divorce lawyer teaming with a forensic accountant.

Forming key partnerships with collaborators allows you to add auxiliary services or products to your offering without your having to learn a new skill. It also helps boost your brand and increase your reach to your collaborators' audience while you do the same for them.

When you develop relationships through networking, you can identify other businesses that not only have the same ideal client but are ones you genuinely like and trust—which can lead to successful partnerships for a single project and beyond.

CONTRACTORS

Contractors have something you need—a resource that's necessary to your business. Printing, bookkeeping, legal services, branding work—all of these are crucial business support services. Networking with contractors is the opposite of networking with connectors. Good contractors will work to earn your trust through their interactions with you. Pay attention.

With the easy accessibility of information online, vetting a contractor through their website, reviews, and social media is one thing. Meeting them in person and having unfettered access to ask questions and get a feel for how they do business is another. Take advantage of that! In my experience, when I find a contractor through networking and get to know them on a more personal level (know, like, trust), the service they provide me exceeds anything I might have found through a recommendation alone. (And, yes, I absolutely go home and Google them to find out more. Due diligence, people!)

CLIENTS

Without a doubt, we need to keep an eye out for potential clients when we network, always remembering *networking isn't sales.* Which means that the conversations we have with potential clients during networking activities won't look like sales conversations. A networking event is not the time to pull out your marketing collateral or start quoting prices or draft a contract. Nope.

But that doesn't mean that conversations you have at networking events can't lead to sales conversations. In fact, the conversations you have during a networking event can help lay the groundwork for more productive sales discussions later. This is your opportunity to shine, to ask questions, and to be open and receptive to what your potential client is saying. Listen for their pain points, the things that matter to them, their motivations. People are usually more forthcoming about what's really going on when they don't feel they're being sold to.

At the same time, these more casual get-to-know-you dialogues can help you determine if a person is a good fit for you as a client. If you really bond with someone over a cocktail or networking activity, the odds that you'll form a good provider-client relationship are equally positive. Likewise, if someone irritates the hell out of you in a one-on-one meeting, think twice about taking them on as a client. As Oprah said, "When someone shows you who they are, believe them."

How do you know if someone is actually a real, live, potential client? Listen. Remember when my friend who invited me for the coffee-that-was-just-a-coffee-and-not-a-job-offer said, "Tell me more about what you do"? That wasn't a signal that he was open to a sales conversation (yes, I know that now). But, if they say, "What does it look like to work with you?" or "What do your clients typically get out of working with you?" or "Do you help your clients with [Fill in the Blank]?" they're probably most likely receptive to a sales conversation. And if they ask, "How much does it cost to work with you?" you're definitely on your way!

My friend Katie Myers, a sales strategist, gave me great advice. She suggested that if someone starts to move the chat toward a sales conversation during a first-time meeting (like a networking event), steer them back toward more general topics and tell them, "I just want to focus on getting to know each other today. Let's schedule another time to talk about my services." I like that approach because it allows you to connect in a nonsalesy way to start building that "know, like, and trust" factor now, while setting the intention for a clearly defined sales conversation at a time in the near future.

If you think your potential client is open to a sales conversation, schedule one before you leave their company. Don't wait!

COOL KIDS

Okay. Up 'til now, I've been all "awareness this" and "purpose that." But now I'm going to break character. Because, sometimes, you just want to hang with the Cool Kids.

Cool Kids are people who don't have an obvious relationship to your business goals and objectives. They haven't said anything or done anything that's made you think that they could be a Connector, Collaborator, Contractor, or Client.

You just think they're cool.

They have good energy. You like their laugh. They're funny. They smell good. Whatever it is, you're attracted to them in some way, and you want to take the relationship further.

Have at it.

Make a date for coffee. See what develops. Maybe that person will be your new best friend outside of business. Maybe they end up being your biggest investor. Who knows? Sometimes the Universe nudges us in a direction, and we just go with it.

But.

Be aware of why you're connecting with them. If you enjoy their company and want to be part of their squad, great! But recognize that. Understand that you're investing time in a relationship that may not assist in your business objectives (probably not, since there's no indication at the outset that it will).

By being aware of that, you're able to let go of the "shoulds" and enjoy your time with the Cool Kid. You know you're there just because—that it has no bearing on your business and that that's okay. Later, when you look back at your networking activities and track the results, you won't bang your head against a wall because you "did all the things" with no result. You'll know you chose to build a personal relationship, or even a new friendship, and you can celebrate that. Heck, we can all celebrate friendships!

Networking is about relationships. Relationships are about people. Those people who can identify and organize the people they meet into one of the five categories (Connectors, Collaborators, Contractors, Clients, and Cool Kids) and learn to leverage those relationships to achieve their business goals are the people who get the greatest results from their networking efforts

Prompts and Activities

- Who is an ideal Connector for your business? (and for what businesses are you the ideal Connector?)

- Who is an ideal Collaborator for your business? (and for what businesses are you the ideal Collaborator?)

- What types of Contractors do you need to meet to help you in your business?

- Who is an ideal Client for your business?

- Which of the Five Cs is most important for you to meet, based on your current goals and objectives?

VOLUNTEERING AS NETWORKING

My great-grandfather, H. Boone Johnson, opened a furniture store in McKinney, Texas, in 1928, and he became the first of four generations of entrepreneurs in my family. I was raised to understand that being small-business owners in a small town came with a significant amount of recognition, as well as the responsibility to be of service to the community.

My Grandpa (who took over the store from H. Boone) was a master networker. He was a deacon in his church, ran the war-bond drive in his town during World War II, and was a Scoutmaster for the Boy Scouts. He was also a Lion (no, not *that* kind of lion), a Mason, and a member of both the local chamber of commerce and the Rotary Club. He firmly established a tradition of service in our family—one that I try to carry on today.

While I love sharing the story of my predecessors, I do have a point. And that point is that networking goes beyond defined networking groups. As we've already covered, networking is about building relationships, and we humans are hardwired to make those necessary connections. Anytime we join a group or a cause, we're naturally connecting with other humans for a common purpose.

When you volunteer in civic and community causes, you earn significant social capital that can pay off in many ways—including in your business.

When you engage in civic groups, community organizations, or other cause-related activities, you're bound to form lasting relationships that expand both your personal and professional networks. By contributing to civic and community causes, you earn significant social capital that can pay off in many ways—including in your business.

In the spirit of keeping our conversation focused on awareness, purpose, and intent, I'd like to share a few tips that will help you maximize the time (resource!) you invest in your community service.

I tend to volunteer my time in groups that are at least somewhat aligned with my business. For instance, I was very active in my PTA when my kids were younger. I maintained the group's website and social media, did event planning, and served on the board. I was even president for two years. Let me tell you, the social capital I gained with the school administration and principals paid off in spades until my kiddos left that school.

What it also did was raise my profile and recognition in the community overall. See, I got involved in the PTA immediately after our last move, when I was new to the community and hadn't found my support system yet. Unlike our friend Bob, I joined the tribe, and then *I contributed like crazy* so that I could build the relationships I needed to survive socially and emotionally in my new home.

While I'm not necessarily recommending that everyone go out and take on the presidency of their local PTA, I will tell you that my experience in doing so solidified my place in my new community. No threat of lions for me. No sirree, Bob (as my Grandpa would say).

What did it mean for my business, you ask? Well, I went from being a stranger (red alert!) to someone who knew a lot of people fairly quickly. And, those people thought I was pretty cool (or pretty crazy) to have taken on the presidency, so my social capital was solid. And, because my social capital was solid, I earned a lot of goodwill (a.k.a., people liked me). People knew me, people liked me, people trusted me. Sounding familiar? People want to do business with people they know, like, and trust. By earning those through my service to the PTA, I started to get referrals from all sorts of people. I got my best client as a referral from a local pediatrician *whom I'd never even met* because a school parent referred me to her. So random, but it proves my point.

Currently, I give my time and talents as a career coach to a local food bank. Every month or so, I help their clients who are determined to get off assistance and reenter the job force through goal setting, updating their resume, identifying opportunities, or researching skills training options. This type of work perfectly aligns with my business strategy skills.

I also volunteer with the local high school after-prom committee. Our after-prom event is famous for its scope, and the planning takes an entire school year. It's a huge community event and attracts a lot of volunteers, parents and nonparents alike. For the past few years, I've offered my time to manage the committee's social media channels and design the visitor program for the night of the event. It's something I can do easily, and (again) it aligns perfectly with my skill set.

Both of these volunteer gigs tap into my unique talents and interests, and the time requirements suit my schedule. And, I just feel better when I'm doing something in my community.

Plus (here comes the not-so-selfless part), I live in a fairly small town. We only have two high schools and a few major charities, one of which is the food bank, where I donate time. Guess who's on the board of the food bank. Yep. Some of the biggest local business leaders are offering *their* time and talents to help guide the activities of that nonprofit. And, guess who sponsors the after-prom party at one of the schools. Yep. The same movers and shakers in our little town.

When I show up at the nonprofit or call a local business for sponsorship information, I'm meeting and connecting with people who can be beneficial to my business. And, because we share an interest and are working on the same causes, they automatically credit me with the social capital that elevates me and my business in their eyes.

The nonprofits win, my community wins, my reputation wins, my business wins. It's a win-win-win-win situation.

How can you make community service work for you and your business? Find an opportunity that aligns with your business objectives. (Hello! Awareness, purpose, intent!) Are you a dog trainer? Volunteer your time training dogs at the local shelter. Are you a social media consultant? Offer to manage the social media channels of an organization you admire. I have one client with an aviation repair company who volunteers his time with other pilots to fly donated goods to rural areas of the state for our service veterans. The key here is to find a group in which you can use your time and talents, and through which you gain exposure to the right people to support your business, either as referrals (for example, shelter staff who could recommend you to the *forever families who adopt the shelter dogs*) or as potential clients (other volunteer pilots *who need repairs on their own airplanes*).

One of the best ways to fast-track recognition and social capital is to volunteer for a leadership position either at a nonprofit or a civic organization. As someone who has served on several volunteer boards, I can attest to the fact that the people who step up to lead distinguish themselves from other volunteers. Every time I've thrown my name in the hat to lead a committee or serve on a board, I've seen a corresponding jump in both my business and the number of valuable connections I've made. Yes, the time commitment is generally higher, but so is the reward.

There are a ton of nonprofits and civic organizations that need volunteers. VolunteerMatch.org is an excellent way to connect with a huge variety of nonprofits and volunteer opportunities. But, in general, here are a few types of local organizations with which you might consider sharing your time and talents.

CHAMBERS OF COMMERCE

In addition to leads groups and strictly networking events, chambers of commerce frequently have committees that deal with topics such as the environment, development, legislation, health, education, policy, and more.

PTAS

The PTA on which I served as president had an annual operating budget of about $150,000, and our largest fundraiser attracted more than 300 families and grossed $50,000. We're not talking small events or chump change. Volunteering your time not only raises your social profile but can help you gain valuable skills and project experience, such as in event planning or fundraising efforts. Not into fundraising? PTA board members also manage multiple committees, volunteers, programming, finances, and events. Come on, do it for the kids!

CIVIC NETWORKING GROUPS

Don't overlook the kind of good, old-fashioned groups my grandpa engaged in. Rotary, Kiwanis, Optimist, Lions Clubs (the ones with the beanies, not the manes), Elks—these types of groups are (mostly) nondenominational, service-oriented, and typically frequented by the movers and shakers in a community. If you're willing to give a little of your time, the return on your investment can be exponential.

NONPROFITS

Perusing VolunteerMatch.org recently, I found the following volunteer opportunities: docent at the local children's museum; tool library volunteer at our local makerspace; garden volunteer; search and rescue volunteer; hearing and vision screening volunteer at local schools; IT data volunteer; and about 12 other pages I didn't quite get to. All for nonprofits. All within 20 minutes of my house. Suffice to say, there's an opportunity for everyone, and a little research can turn up some truly fun and rewarding ways to donate your time and talents.

PRO-BONO WORK

This one is kind of a mash-up of everything I've presented thus far, but consider donating your professional services through skill-based volunteering and pro-bono work. While I don't advocate that my clients make a habit of giving away their services, I do encourage them to consider working with people or projects that will develop their skills and knowledge, and to count that personal and professional development as a nonmonetary reward for their services.

If you choose to donate your products or services, record the time spent on pro-bono work and track the fees and expenses of any associated projects as if they were being completed for paying clients. One reason for this is that you can actually write off some donations of goods and services as tax deductions. The other reason is to foster awareness about how you're *really* spending your time and how much value you're donating, and to calculate the ROI of your volunteering efforts.

I'm the first one to promote volunteering—both for business and personal reasons. But, as I emphasized earlier, any time we spend away from our business is an investment, so I encourage you to invest it wisely. If you're using volunteering as a way to further your business goals, track, record, and evaluate your activities so that you can be aware, purposeful, and intentional about your actions and their results.

Later in this book, I'll share some simple tracking tips you can use to organize and record the results of your networking efforts. Connections you make through volunteering are no different.

Note the people you meet, the conversations you have, and any tangible or nontangible benefits to your business gained through your volunteer work with nonprofits or community organizations.

Regardless of where you choose to donate your time and talents, use the same criteria to evaluate whether it's a good fit for you and your business. Be aware of your reason for joining or volunteering in a particular group. And be purposeful and intentional about what you hope to accomplish by being there. There's no right or wrong answer—only the right answer for you and your business. And, in this case, for the community you're serving.

Prompts and Activities

- Which civic groups exist in your community? Make plans to visit the ones most likely to fit your goals and interests.

- Do you have goods and/or services you could donate to a nonprofit in exchange for sponsorship recognition?

- What volunteer opportunities exist in your community that align with your interests and goals? Call the volunteer coordinators of the groups that pique your interest to ask how you can serve.

HELLO
my name is
Chapter 9

BE ALL IN

If you're like me, the time requirements for successful net-working can be daunting. Every networking event takes us away from the "real work" we do. Add in our social anxieties and it's far too easy to convince ourselves that we just don't have the time.

Successful small-business owners will tell you, though, that they got to where they are today because of the people who helped them along the way. A strong professional network can help your business in a million ways, including helping you find great employees and consultants, offering peer advice or strategic partnerships, and either helping you generate leads or by becoming clients themselves.

But, as I've said several (many) times throughout this book, successful networking takes time. Time to build the mutually beneficial relationships that will help you and your business grow. Time to allow people to get to know, like, and trust you enough that they also want to support you.

The more time you spend networking, the more successful you'll be, as long as you're doing it with awareness, purpose, and intent. Be aware of your objectives for networking, be purposeful about where and how you spend your networking resources (Time! Money!), and be intentional about building the right connections with the right people to help you achieve those goals.

Just a reminder: A recent survey showed that business owners who said networking played a role in their success spent an average of 6.3 hours a week doing it, whereas business owners who said networking did *not* play a role in their success averaged less than two hours a week engaging in networking activities. People, you reap what you sow!

By the way, if you're sitting at home thinking to yourself, "Great! I just need to up my game to 6.3 hours a week of networking," consider this: people who networked 20 hours a week claimed 70 percent of their business came from networking and referrals.

Twenty. Hours.

How do you leverage your precious, precious time wisely? We've already talked about the types of networking groups that might work for you and your business, but now let's dig a little deeper. When you're planning your networking activities, ignore your people, get involved in a big way, and be all in.

IGNORE YOUR PEOPLE

What I mean is, don't spend all your time networking with people who are in the same industry as you. I actually see this a lot. We choose groups that are populated by people similar to us because we're more comfortable there. It's a safe space. The other members sound like us, and they talk like us. They understand the industry-speak being bantered about. They can commiserate with other attendees about business challenges.

But guess what. People who do the same thing as you aren't going to buy your services.

When I network, I look for groups that bring together a variety of industries and disciplines, because that's where I'm more likely to meet Connectors, Collaborators, Contractors, and Clients. ("What about Cool Kids?" I can hear you asking. Pffftt! Cool Kids are *everywhere!*)

GET INVOLVED IN A BIG WAY

Many organizations and groups have advisory boards or elected officers to help run things. Although it does increase the time investment on your part, there's an equal boost in your visibility within the group when you take on a leadership role.

Consider this: If you've been purposeful about joining groups and attending events populated by your clients and potential clients, and you're consistently positioned and introduced as one of the leaders within the organization, you gain an incredible boost to your brand. Not only do you create name recognition (you're listed in the program and on the website, and you're introduced at various events), but you also develop a strong reputation as an expert. The perception among members of any organization is that the people tapped to lead are the most capable and best suited for the job. The trust factor goes through the roof.

By getting heavily involved in the right organization, you'll also build social cred. People see how hard those in leadership work, and they'll see how well you work when you're at your best. The associations formed "under fire" as part of the leadership team will result in stronger business relationships.

The exposure benefits of being a leader can't be overlooked, either. WEBO Network positions our Advisory Board as the leaders within the organization, and they get additional marketing and promotion benefits. Many other organizations do the same. Another compelling reason to step up!

BE ALL IN

I wish (oh, how I wish) that I could tell you there are shortcuts to networking. But, alas, there are not. It takes time. A lot of time. And you, dear reader, have to be the one taking the time to do it. You have to get out from behind your desk and make those connections. No one is as passionate and articulate about your brand as you are. So, truly, you need to be the one out there sharing it with the world.

I once attended a local chapter of an international networking organization. This particular group had a strict attendance policy, but it did allow members to send proxies when they were personally unable to attend. The proxies were there to deliver someone else's elevator speech. If, however, there were no competing businesses in the room, they were invited to introduce themselves during the guest portion of the event. A proxy (we'll call her Bobby Sue) stood up and pulled out her iPad with the missing attendee's elevator pitch on it. She read it in a monotone. She sat down. I have absolutely no recollection of anything she shared.

I don't remember the missing attendee's name.

I don't remember the missing attendee's business or the value they could have offered me.

I don't even remember the proxy's name.

All I remember is how weird I thought the whole thing was.

A client once called for my opinion. As a small, locally owned business, he recognized that networking could be a huge asset to growing his brand. *But* (a big one), he didn't want to take the time to do it himself. He was looking at hiring a networking consultant (permanent proxy) to do his networking for him. And he thought this was a *fabulous* idea.

Excuse me?

Then another client in a different market called with the same plan because he'd heard it from the first client and he thought it was a great idea!

Shoot me now.

I understand hiring a sales rep to go out into the world and pimp your business. But (say it with me) *networking isn't sales.* Networking is building a relationship. *You* are the face of your business. *You* are your brand's best champion. You want those relationships to be with *you*, not some stand-in. Remember, people get to know you when *you* show up.

Please. Be all in. Commit the time. Show up.

Prompts and Activities

- Do any of the groups or organizations you participate in have open leadership positions?

- How can you best leverage your time and talents to increase your recognition within the groups to which you belong?

- Are there any groups in which you hold membership that no longer serve your goals and objectives?

- Are there groups that you've joined that you no longer enjoy? (Note: Many groups have multiple meeting times and days, so before quitting altogether, consider checking out other meetings to see if those are more your style. After all, you've invested time and money. Don't throw in the towel until you're sure it's no longer a good fit!)

HAVE YOUR SH*T TOGETHER

We've already talked about how many business owners fall victim to the "shoulds." They know they *should* be networking, so, gosh darn it, they're gonna get out there and network! They log in to Meetup.com or their local chamber of commerce page, find a group or event, and off they go. Determined to work that net.

Which is all well and good if they've figured out their "why" for networking—their purpose for doing it—and they've been intentional about choosing that group or event they're headed off to.

Let's assume they've read this book and that they have, indeed, defined their reason for wanting to network. They understand how networking is going to support their overall business goals and objectives. They've identified the resources (Time! Money!) they have available to them, and they've been intentional about the type of group that best suits their purpose. They've written out and practiced, practiced, practiced their elevator speech (more on this later). Good job, business owner!

Off goes our little business owner, ready to make connections.

Now, if you know me, you know I have a mantra that I live by. Grab your highlighter, because here it is:

You have to look like you have your sh*t together.

Why?

Audiences make eight judgments about you within eight seconds of seeing you, including opinions about your self-esteem, self-respect, confidence, organizational skills, soundness of judgment, attention to detail, creativity, and reliability.

Did you know that audiences make eight judgments about you within eight seconds of seeing you? Those eight conclusions include opinions about your self-esteem, self-respect, confidence, organizational skills, soundness of judgment, attention to detail, creativity, and reliability.

Think about that. In eight seconds, people are judging you on your ability to organize, make good decisions, and be reliable. Those are exactly the kinds of qualities clients are looking for when they're shopping for new products and services.

Eight. Seconds.

What I always tell my clients is, people trust people who look like they have their sh*t together. And, people give money to people they trust. So, if we want to get their money (business), we have to look like we have our sh*t together. And, we've got eight seconds do to it.

It's just another way of saying we want people to know, like, and trust us.

What does it look like to have your sh*t together in networking? In this chapter and the next, I'm going to share some specific things you can do to prepare yourself before an event, things you can do during an event, and things you can after an event to impress the hell out of people and—yes—look like you have your sh*t together.

DO YOUR RESEARCH

Once you've identified the right group for your business objectives, slip into your stalker persona and start stalking.

Visit the group's Eventbrite/Meetup/Facebook Event pages and look through pictures of past events. What are people wearing? What does the seating arrangement look like? What types of comments are there about the last get-together? Join the discussion and post a question about what you can expect from the occasion.

If their details are available, reach out to the facilitator or hostess. Introduce yourself and ask what you can expect. Is there anything you should prepare for the event?

If you can't do your stalking ahead of time, then go with a look-and-see attitude. Maybe play it a little quieter the first time you're there, and sit back and observe the networking culture, because every event and every group does it a little differently. You want to make sure that you're blending into that culture and not sticking out in a way that lets the lions get too close.

MAKE A PLAN

The same sites that allow you to get a read on the event before you go also give you an opportunity to scope out who will be there. Read through the RSVP list to see who is planning to attend. Is there anyone you know? Is there anyone in particular you'd like to know? Who are the Connectors, Collaborators, Contractors, Clients, and Cool Kids on the list? To whom do you want to introduce yourself when you get there? To whom could you introduce yourself before you go?

Make a plan for the people with whom you want to connect, including why you want to connect with them, and what you want the outcome of that connection to be. Tweak your elevator speech for the audience and event, and work out what your call to action will be for this particular occasion. Because you've done your research, prepare any additional materials that you might be invited to present or leave on a display.

Be aware of your objectives for attending so that you can be purposeful about the connections you make there and intentional in leveraging those connections to achieve your goals.

HAVE A BUSINESS CARD

I can feel you rolling your eyes at me (seriously, I'm the mother of two teens, I can feel that sh*t a mile away). "Duh," I hear you thinking, "of course I'll have a business card!"

Oh, sure, you say that now. And then you run out of cards and forget to order them. Or, you change purses and forget to put more cards in the new bag.

I can't tell you how many networking events I go to where somebody stands up and says, "I didn't bring any business cards today." Well, friend, how am I supposed to find you later? People don't like to think, so don't assume that other attendees will diligently write down your name, go home, Google you, track down your contact details, and invite you to connect. Not. Going. To. Happen. If you go in without a card, you might as well not go in at all (okay, maybe a little extreme, but you get my point).

Take lots of business cards. In fact, take your box of business cards out of your desk drawer and put them in your car. Right now. Go. I'll wait.

Have. A. Business. Card.

BUTTON UP YOUR ONLINE PRESENCE

What's the first thing you do when you meet someone at a networking event? If you're like me, you go home and start looking at their website and their social media to learn more about them and their business. This is especially true if I'm targeting them *before* an event or if I schedule a follow-up one-on-one meeting after the event.

Knowing this, it's imperative that your online presence present you in the best possible light. Keep your website updated and ensure that all your forms and opt-ins are current and in working order. Review your social media profiles to make sure all your links are working and the information is up to date. Post consistently on your social media channels so that visitors have an introduction to your brand and voice.

If you have a current offer or program, update your header images across all your social media channels for consistency. Update your headshot regularly and use the same one (or one of a series) on every channel to build brand recognition. How you present yourself online plays a significant role in how people will perceive your professionalism, reliability, and expertise. Make it good.

In business, perception is everything. How we carry ourselves professionally, how we present ourselves professionally, and how we interact with other professionals tells our clients and potential clients what they can expect from us and our business. It's our brand, and our brand is a promise that we make based on that expectation and perception.

By taking the time to create a plan, do your research, prepare yourself, and present yourself in a purposeful and intentional way, you create a consistent, cohesive image. Believe me, people notice. When you care about your appearance and how you show up, they know that means you'll care about the work you do with them.

I always say, people admire people who have their sh*t together. Earn the admiration (like) and respect (trust) of those with whom you want to build those mutually beneficial relationships that will help you and your business grow.

Prompts and Activities

- Order an extra box of business cards and store it in your car.

- What products and services could you be sharing during your networking engagements? Use your marketing calendar and plan ahead.

- Take time (or hire a social media consultant) to audit your website and social media channels to ensure you're putting your best digital face forward.

YOUR ELEVATOR SPEECH

It's a widely held belief that the number-one fear people have is public speaking (even above death).[8] I say "belief" because it's hard to find scientific studies to support that claim. Some older surveys show that snakes are our top fear, whereas more recent ones show that corruption and man-made disasters top the list. But, to be fair, fear of public speaking is always ranked among the top nail-biters.

The fact that speaking in front of people is so often touted as being the list-topper does demonstrate the hold that glossophobia (fear of public speaking) has on our collective psyches.

Which is why I have a bone to pick with the guy or gal who coined the term "elevator *speech*." Ugh! Talk about setting us up to fail.

If you're not familiar with the elevator speech—sometimes called "your elevator pitch"—here's the theory. Say you get into an elevator with another person to go up 20 floors. That person, against all social norms, engages you in conversation and asks what you do (hey, buddy, you're supposed to stand silently facing forward and watch the lights on the panel change). An elevator climbs an average of one floor every 1.5 seconds, so you have 30 seconds to say who you are, what you do, and whom you serve. According to the theory, after giving your speech, that person should have all the information necessary to decide whether to buy your service or product.

GO! (No pressure.)

When you stop and think about it, standing up in front of a group of strangers, speaking, and sharing not only what you do but who you serve and how you serve them in a compelling, concise manner is a big ask. It's no wonder that those 30 to 60 seconds can strike such fear in the hearts of men and women alike. The whole scenario taps into the evolutionary fears of being rejected and of doing something that will get you ostracized from the group. There you are, all by your lonesome. With a big, bright (albeit imaginary) spotlight shining down on you.

What if you say something wrong?

What if you have spinach in your teeth?

What if the other people in the room reject you?

I mean, the lions come for the stragglers, so when we stand up, alone, in front of everyone, we put ourselves directly within the reach of those giant teeth and claws.

Geez.

(But, again, no pressure!)

Elevator speeches are frequently associated with those (excruciating) 30 to 60 seconds when you stand in front of a room full of people to introduce yourself. But, actually, it applies to any time you're asked "What do you do?" So, yeah, it could actually be in an elevator. Or at a networking after-hours. Or at an interview.

Whether you're asked to give it in front of a room full of people, or at a smaller table within the larger group, or to an individual you meet at the lobby bar, your elevator speech is, quite simply, how you introduce yourself. It comes in all shapes and sizes and lengths.

Regardless of where you're delivering it—over a cocktail, into a microphone, or in that elevator—every elevator speech needs to convey the same information. This includes:

- Who you are
- What you do
- Who you serve
- What problems you solve for them

When I work with my clients on their elevator speeches, one of the things I hear most is "I just don't know what to say!"

Really? Let me ask you a couple questions:

Do you know your name? (Gonna assume the answer here is yes.) Check!

Do you know the name of your business? (Again, going with yes here.) Check!

Friend, you're one-quarter of the way to a successful elevator speech! Now, we just have to work on the rest of it.

Your elevator speech is a short-and-sweet version of your brand promise. And your brand promise is just that: a *promise*. It's what those people who come in contact with you and your business can be assured that you'll deliver. Your brand promise is the essence of your overall brand. It's what motivates clients in your direction. When you summarize your brand promise into your elevator speech or introduction, you instantly give potential customers an idea about what they can expect from you and your business, and you can begin to nudge them toward those sales conversations we talked about earlier.

When we start to talk about brand, my toes get all tingly and my eyes light up. This is the nut of business, people. This is the *thing* that, once we define, understand, and embrace it will change everything in our business. From our marketing messages to the products and services we offer. From the people we hire to the systems and procedures we put into place. It's *everything.*

When a client says to me "I don't know what to say!" I instantly know there's a deeper issue at play than just a 30-second elevator speech. If you aren't able to tell people—either individually or in front of room full of humans—who you are, what you do, whom you serve, and how you help them, then we need to back up and create some solid definitions for you to be able to move forward successfully.

Your brand is what differentiates you from every other business providing a similar product or service. I say "similar" because no one does it exactly the way you do. It's those little (or big) distinctions that set you apart from your competition and make you shine to your ideal client like a lighthouse through the fog. By being able to articulate those differences to your audience, you'll immediately help them place you in their own sphere of understanding. "She does *this* to help *that* kind of client. Got it!"

Having a profound understanding of your brand—what makes you different, unique, and special—also helps you interact more confidently in a networking situation. How many times have you gone to a new group only to find that they have four other mortgage brokers/dog groomers/tomato growers in the group, and you've thought to yourself, "This isn't the group for me. She's already here and she's already got all the business in this room"?

Guess what. You're different from her. You grow a different strain of tomatoes. The dogs in your grooming room get organic treats instead of mass-market nummies. You specialize in securing mortgages for unicyclists. Whatever it is, whether it's your product, your service, or your ideal client, there's something about you that sets you apart from every other business in the same industry.

When you know what makes you different and sets you apart, you can stand up and introduce yourself in a way that shines a light on that difference for everyone in the room. It helps people who don't know about tomatoes or dog grooming or home financing for unicyclists understand that there are differences within your industry and that you might be a better fit for their organic-tomato-loving unicyclist uncle than the lady over there.

In order for you to get to that deep understanding of your uniqueness, you have to ask yourself some deep questions. It's not enough to ask yourself what you do. You also have to ask yourself (sometimes more than once) *how you're different from anyone else.*

Let me show you what I mean.

WHO YOU ARE

We're starting off with the easy stuff here.

Who are you? Keep it simple. Name. Business name.

"Hi, I'm Katherine McGraw Patterson. Most people call me KP. I'm a business strategist, speaker, and founder of WEBO Network."

Done and dusted.

Moving on....

WHAT YOU DO

Okay, I just told you that your brand is all about how unique you are, and how different and special you and your business are. And, you are. You're different, and unique, and special!

But, right now. For this section. Just here. I want you to be like everyone else.

"What?!?!?!" (oh, I can hear your exclamations from here) "I don't *want* to be like everyone else!"

Yes, yes, I know. But, here's the deal. People need to be able to define and understand who you are. They need to be able to hear your elevator speech and think, "Right-o, she does *this* for *that* type of customer." The have to recognize easily what it is that you offer so that they can catalog you into the right space in their universe.

We don't want to be stereotyped by any means. But if we don't give people a clear reference point in terms of who we are and what we do, they're going to be confused. They won't "get" us. If they don't understand us, they can't tell other people about how great we are.

For example, I live in an area of the world that's saturated with coaches, spiritual healers, and energy workers. I've literally heard these introductions:

- I am a desire magnetizer.
- I am an advocate for the goddess.
- I am a brand warrior.
- I am an innovation guru.
- I am a technology evangelist.

I'm going to out myself now. In my marketing communications business, I call myself "Chief Creative Strategist" (insert cry-laughing emoji here).

Well, now, aren't we all just so pretty?

Listen, you're awesome. I know you've spent a lifetime building your expertise and studying your craft. You're passionate about what you do. You live it. You love it.

But I don't understand what you do.

Some people call it "jargon." Another author I read called it "airy-fairy" (love that). I call it "industry-speak." Call it what you will, but we all use it from time to time. It's a super-specific lingo that people in our own unique industries use to communicate with each other. It's a secret handshake that (guess what) *no one else knows.*

So, please, don't use it in your elevator speech. Keep your fancy-schmancy industry-speak to yourself.

People need to know who you are and what you do. You only have 30 to 60 seconds to tell them. Don't leave anything to their imagination.

Here are some examples of how to share what you do:

- I am a business coach who helps entrepreneurs get more clients and make more money.
- I am a systems consultant for businesses that want to find the right automation software to save time.
- I am a health and wellness coach who helps people lose extra weight.
- I am a consultant who helps businesses that are ready to make their first hires.

You want people to understand who you are and what you do so that they know whether they want to connect with you to learn more. Your 30 to 60 seconds have to entice them, inform them, and educate them enough that they can identify if you're a good fit for them or someone they know.

Use these questions to help you create your definition of what you do:

- In one sentence, how would you describe your business?
- What does your business do best?
- How would you describe your products or services?
- Do you think there are clear and distinct differences between your offering and those of your competitors? (service offering, price, personnel, etc.) What are they?

Don't be clever. Don't be creative. Don't make them think (people don't like to think). Make it easy for them. Tell them who you are. Use language everyone understands.

WHOM YOU SERVE

I have this pet peeve. When I'm at a networking event and someone is giving their elevator speech and they say, "I work with anyone who..."

"...anyone who has skin..."

"...anyone who likes money..."

"...anyone who needs a house..."

Oh, FFS. No, you *don't*!

Think about your best clients. Your favorites. The ones who make your heart sing and your cash register ring. The ones you love to serve, for whom you'll gladly go the extra mile. They're not "anyone who..." They're certain types of people or businesses.

Now, think about your least favorite clients. The ones who don't pay on time. The ones who disagree with your findings or insist that you provide extra services outside of your scope. The clients who, when their name shows up on your caller ID, you let go to voicemail and then take your sweet time calling back because you know (you just know) it's going to be something annoying.

Those are the *"anyone who..."* clients.

Let's talk about brand a bit more. Branding can be scary for small-business owners and entrepreneurs because the best brands are exclusive. What do I mean? I mean that the best, most successful brands don't serve everyone. They don't even pretend to try to serve everyone. These brands are unafraid and unapologetic when they say, "You're my person, and you're *not.*"

As business owners, we can fall into the belief that the more people we get our message out to, and the more people we serve, the more money we'll make. And, we're all in business to make money. The fact is, we can't be all things to all people. Especially as solopreneurs and small- business owners. We don't have the bandwidth or the resources (Time! Money!) or the skill set to provide all the things to all the people.

So, we have to choose.

Let me ask you, why did you start your own business? If you're like most of my coaching clients, it's because you wanted more control. More control over your time, more control over the type of work and projects you do, and more control over who you work with. That's really a beautiful thing—to be able to choose with whom we work, both as partners and as clients.

Instead of being afraid to turn people away, I encourage you to celebrate the fact that you get to say no to clients who aren't an ideal fit for you and your business. Because, believe me, the "anyone who..." clients are exhausting!

I'm also going to let you in on a little secret. When you pull up your big-girl panties and get real about both whom you want to serve and whom you're best able to serve, you'll not only enjoy your work more, but *you'll enjoy more work*. Once you become associated with providing an exceptional product or service to a specific clientele, word will get around. Then, it's like that lighthouse shining through the fog again. Your ideal client will flock to your business as the ideal provider for *their* needs.

I won't say it's magical, but it's pretty darn cool when it happens.

Although saying "anyone who..." sounds cute and catchy in an elevator speech, think about it. If you tell me that, and I refer people to you based on your catchall approach to clients, is that beneficial or profitable for you and your business? If the referrals and clients you gain from networking don't aid in your success, then you've wasted your time, money, and energy. As with everything else when networking, being aware of your ideal client, being purposeful about defining that client for your audience, and being intentional about asking for introductions to your ideal client are what will make your networking efforts successful.

There are a bunch of different things you can use to define your ideal client. There are demographics (age, gender, marital status, income), and psychographics (needs, wants, pain points), and practical stuff like their budget for your service. But, when it comes to synopsizing your ideal client in your elevator speech, I want you to tell me such things as whether:

- You serve individuals or businesses
- You serve a specific gender
- You serve people in a specific relationship status
- You serve a specific age range
- You serve clients in a specific location or area

Here's how your answers help me understand more about whom you serve:

- My ideal clients are teens who struggle with acne.
- My ideal clients are newly single moms.
- My ideal clients are married couples.
- My ideal clients are female corporate executives and women in upper-level management.

As I write this section, that an old Lori Morgan song *"Five Minutes"* keeps running through my mind (yes, I love country. I'm from Texas, after all!) in which sweet Lori tells her lover that he had five minutes to do some smooth talking. To tell her what she needed to know to make her decision about whether to stay or go.

Your elevator speech does the same thing for your audience. The difference is that, instead of a whopping five minutes, you have 30 to 60 seconds. The requirements are still the same. You have to tell your audience what they need to hear in order to make up their mind whether to engage with you (stay) or move on (go).

You don't need a miracle to convince your audience of your value, just a clear message that tells them who you are, what you do, and whom you serve. Don't leave them guessing. Their bags are packed and waiting by the door. As Lori said, "figure it out!"

Prompts and Activities

- Create a simple elevator speech using this formula: "Hello, my name is _____. I am a _____. I serve _____ who are looking for _____."

- Next, ask your friends how they'd describe you and what you do.

- Compare their answers to the statement you prepared. Do they match? If not, where are the differences? Which version is most understandable (i.e., doesn't use industry-speak) to someone who doesn't know you or your business?

HELLO
my name is
Chapter 12

DON'T BRING A SALES PITCH, BRING A HOOK
(OR: HOW TO MAKE YOUR ELEVATOR SPEECH WORK FOR YOU)

The goal of networking is to build relationships, so your 30-to-60-second elevator speech isn't a sales pitch. It's your introduction. It's the opening gambit in a series of conversations you'll (hopefully) have with your new contact.

Conversation is defined as "the exchange of ideas by spoken words."

Exchange. Give and take.

Your elevator speech is just the first in a series of conversations.

Your job as the giver of the speech is to offer enough information that it opens the door to future exchanges. The listener's job is to evaluate what you've said and decide if that's a door they want to open.

You create interest and provide data.

They determine what to do with it.

What can you offer to increase the odds that your audience will want to engage with you further? In the last chapter, we covered the basics: who you are, what you do, and whom you serve. Now that you're comfortable with that, let's dig deeper into the problems you solve, because that's where the real interest lies.

THE PROBLEMS YOU SOLVE

What every business does is solve problems. I need or want something you have, I pay you, I get the thing. Problem solved. Simple, yes?

What if I told you that with every transaction you're solving two problems? (1) A practical problem (I need the thing, you sell me the thing, now I have the thing) and (2) an emotional problem (I *want* the thing because it will make me feel a certain way, I buy the thing, I feel a certain way, and my emotional needs are fulfilled). So, when I ask you what you do, I'm asking what you *do* (practical) and what *value* you provide (emotional).

A compelling elevator speech not only tells people what you *do* but also shares the emotional *value* of what you offer.

If you have a hard time identifying the emotional problems you solve for people, think back to your initial conversations with your best clients. What problems did they present to you? What's the exact language they used to describe their situation? Guess what. If you paid attention, they gave you the best language to use when describing what you do for other people. My suggestion is always to incorporate that language in your messaging so that your ideal clients hear and immediately know you're talking to them.

For instance, an aesthetician who works with acne-afflicted teens might hear, "I don't want to go to school looking like this—it's so embarrassing," or "People make fun of my skin." The emotional value of her service (acne treatments) is in both the clear skin and the confidence, self-assurance, and self-acceptance that clear skin gives her clients. Mimicking that language—social ease, self-confidence—will paint a picture of the type of person she serves.

A financial planner who works with newly single moms to organize and set up systems for a family's finances might hear, "My ex-husband always did the checkbook—he said it was too complicated for me" or "I haven't managed finances in years—I was a disaster before I got married and gladly let my ex-husband take over." What she's hearing is that her practical service of helping set up and manage a family's finances alleviates fear and self-doubt. Using that language helps people understand the emotional value her service provides.

If we go back to the "what you do" and "whom you serve" examples I shared earlier, and we add the emotional value of your product or service, it might look like this:

- I'm a business coach who helps entrepreneurs get more clients, make more money, and *feel more in control.*
- I'm a systems consultant for businesses that want to find the right automation software to save time and *reduce overwhelm.*
- I'm a consultant who helps businesses that are ready to make their first hires *be confident* they've found the right candidates.
- I'm an aesthetician who works with teens who struggle with acne so they *feel better* about themselves.

- I'm a financial planner who serves newly single moms who *are nervous* about managing their family's money.

How can you dig deep into the emotional problems you solve for your clients? Use these prompts to get a greater understanding of your value:

- Something has happened to cause your potential clients to look for the types of service/product you offer. Describe their situation.
- What kind of language do they use to describe their goals for buying your product or service?
- What problems can you solve for them? How will your service/product improve their lives?
- Of all the benefits you offer, which are the most important to your ideal clients?

People make decisions based on emotions. When you use emotional language in your elevator speech to describe your ideal client and your services, you create an emotional connection and help your audience understand the reasons why someone would choose you over your competition. It makes it more real.

How many elevator speeches have you heard? A hundred? A thousand? How many do you remember?

The best elevator speeches have a few things in common. One, a hook: something that grabs the audience's attention immediately. Two, social proof: information that shows that what you have to offer fulfills it promises to deliver. And three, a call to action. For 30 to 60 seconds, you have the stage and the attention of the room. Use it by asking them to do something.

YOUR HOOK

You have 30 to 60 seconds to capture your audience's attention. To say something memorable. Odds are, as you stand up to give your introduction, others in the room are passing business cards, sugaring their coffee, turning off their phones, waiting for their turn to speak. Or, they've already zoned out after listening to the first 10 people mumble something about their business.

You need to wow them from the get-go so that they'll listen. Snap them out of their trance. Wake them up. Get them to pay attention to what you have to say.

A "hook" is a statement that doesn't necessarily have anything to do with what you do. It's intended to shake up the discussion so that your listeners can't form any preconceived notion about you and your business.

Although you want the members of your audience to understand what you do so that they can organize you in their mental Rolodex, when you stand up to introduce yourself and say, "Hello, my name is Bob, I'm a software engineer..." be prepared to cue the snores. You can almost hear their brains thinking "...software engineer...yada, yada, yada...heard it before."

A great hook makes your audience sit up and take notice. It makes their brains think, "Wait, what did he just say?" and tune in to find out more.

That's what you want.

"Hold on," I can hear you saying, "you just told me not to get clever with my speech."

Yep. I did.

Back in Chapter 11, I talked about obscure introductions and "anyone who..." statements, and how they can confuse your audience. I'll admit, those are things that sound an awful lot like hooks. The difference is that a hook doesn't confuse your audience. It intrigues them. It's a split-second statement that snaps your audience to attention and tunes them into your *next* statements about who you are, whom you serve, and the value you offer. If you tell me you're the "advocate for the goddess" as a way of explaining yourself, you've lost me. But, if you use that as a hook to grab my attention and follow it right away with: "I'm a life coach who works with women to uncover their strengths to find more satisfaction in their careers," then I can catalog you into my worldview immediately — life coach, works with women, career focus. What could have been a random, confusing statement becomes something that tells me more about you and your personality.

A great hook taps into your ideal client's deepest desires and the emotional problem that you set out to solve for them. (Hint: their deepest desire isn't to have a balanced checkbook, get business coaching, or have their pimples popped).

My go-to hook is "I empower business owners to transform their business." One of my favorite ways to start off my elevator speech is "Hi, I'm KP and I hate networking."

My audience is hooked.

They laugh. They snap to awareness to hear more. I have the attention of the room.

Hooks can be easier (and a bit sassier) when they're delivered to an individual asking you "What do you do?"

"I pop pimples for a living." (an aesthetician)

"I get you where you're going." (an auto broker)

"I pay for the things you break." (an insurance broker)

Again, a great hook's purpose is to pique your audience's curiosity and grab their attention. When it's delivered one on one in private conversation, it should lead your listener to ask, "What do you mean?" and open the door to a deeper discussion. When it's delivered to a group, it should help you cut through the noise (literal and figurative) of the room and engage peoples' interest so that they'll approach you to learn more.

One caveat: you don't want to sound cheesy when you deliver your hook, so delivery is key.

MAKE YOUR ELEVATOR SPEECH WORK FOR YOU

Let's say you're in a networking event of 30 people, which is not unheard of. At most, you'll connect with three to five key people (Connectors, Collaborators, Contractors, Clients, or Cool Kids). Those conversation will allow you to move your relationship closer to a sales conversation.

But what about the other 25 people?

You have 30 to 60 seconds in your elevator speech to wow your audience. To command the stage and their attention. You might never have that chance again. How can you use it as productively as possible?

If the base of your elevator speech (who you are, what you do, whom you serve) is the ice cream, and the emotional value you add is the whipped cream on top, let me tell you about the sprinkles! Social proof and a nifty call to action. Yummy!

Social proof

You're walking along the street and you think to yourself, "Hey, I'd really like an ice cream cone right about now." And there in front of you are two ice cream parlors. One has a line out the door and down the street. One is empty. Which do you choose?

You hop in line. The wait doesn't deter you, because, obviously, it must be the tastier choice, right? All these other people wouldn't be waiting so long if it weren't.

That's a powerful dynamic we used to call "word-of-mouth." I like to call it "herd mentality" (cuz I'm from Texas). Today's psychologists, sociologists, and new media marketers call it "social proof." Basically, "social proof" means we assume the actions of others are the correct behaviors.

You may not realize it, but I've been using social proof throughout this book. Every time I say "my clients" or share an anecdote about an experience, I'm showing you that other people have followed my advice and succeeded. Therefore, it's safe for you to accept what I'm saying as the correct behavior.

Other examples of social proof include:
- Testimonials on your website
- Follower counts on social media
- Bouncers who delay entry so that long and visible lines form in front of the club, driving up interest

How do you use social proof in your elevator speech? Brag a bit. Don't be afraid to share your successes or name drop to get your audience to believe that your product or service is the right choice for their needs. Here are five ways you can incorporate social proof into your introduction:

1. **Statistics:** More than half my clients are able to retire within 10 years of our beginning work together.
2. **Anecdotes:** My client Bob's skin cleared up so well that he just won America's Next Top Model!
3. **Celebrities:** Oprah brings her dogs to be groomed at our doggie spa.
4. **Experts:** Four out of five unicyclists recommend our mortgage service to their friends.
5. **Real time:** Saying something that shows the people in your audience that they need your product, such as "Who here likes money?" (Note: This approach can be risky, so make sure you ask a question guaranteed to get a strong response!)

Call to action

"What a shame." That's what I think to myself when I hear someone deliver an elevator speech that doesn't ask me to do something. You've just given me great information about who you are, what you do, and whom you serve. You've helped me connect emotionally with your business. And now? What do you want me to do with that?

What's the response you want after your elevator speech? Just as there are lots of reasons to network, there are lots of things to ask for. Do you want:

- Referrals?
- An appointment for a presentation?
- Information?
- Resources?
- Job leads?
- Investors?
- Something else?

Your call to action, like other components of your elevator speech, will vary based on the situation in which you present it. When you're aware of your purpose for being in a group or at an event, you can be purposeful and intentional about asking your audience for what you want.

We're spending a lot of time on your elevator speech because it's often the first impression your audience will have of you and your business. First impressions are important. Remember those eight things people assume about you in the first eight seconds of meeting you? Let me refresh your memory. In those eight seconds, they're making judgments about your self-esteem, self-respect, confidence, organizational skills, soundness of judgment, attention to detail, creativity, and reliability.

In eight seconds, people are forming an opinion about you and your business. And that opinion will help them decide whether they want to continue a conversation with you beyond your first meeting. Networking is about having those conversations and building those relationships. A great introduction will help position you to make that happen.

Ooh, I can see you sweating from here. Remember when we talked about our fears of public speaking? I feel your anxiety! You're already edgy about standing up in front of people to speak, and now I'm telling you how good you have to be doing it.

I also told you that I'd help you create systems and strategies to take the emotional sting out of networking. Let me do that. Visit LunchingwithLions.com to download fill-in-the-blank templates and handy tips you can use to create that compelling and engaging introduction that will entice your new contacts to take the discussion further.

Over the past couple of chapters, I've asked you to define your brand components: who you are, what you do, whom you serve, and what problems you solve. If you didn't answer the questions in those sections, I encourage you to go back now and spend some time really thinking about your responses. Because now we're going to take that information and craft it into your elevator speech.

TIPS

Since embarking on my personal networking challenge, not only have I crafted my own elevator speech (which I continue to tweak and polish), but I've seen hundreds, if not thousands, of other business owners deliver theirs. In WEBO Network, we dedicate at least one meeting each year to delivering and evaluating each other's pitches so that we can get better and more comfortable in our delivery.

I've seen good pitches, and I've seen really, really bad pitches. The kind that make you cringe for the person delivering it. In watching all those introductions, I've come up with some tips to help make your delivery better. Here they are:

- **Be customer-centric:** Limit your use of "I" and focus on what you offer your customers. What's their deepest desire? How does your product or service change their lives for the better?
- **Keep it short and sweet:** Nothing's worse than being asked by the hostess to keep your introduction to 30 seconds and then have someone drone on and on for several minutes. Be respectful of others' time.
- **Edit, then edit, then edit again:** Learn to read the room when you deliver your introduction and pay attention to

audience reactions to parts of your speech. Use that as a guide to help you refine your content and your delivery. As I said, I'm continually tweaking and polishing my introduction to make it better, more concise, and more engaging.

- **Skip the industry jargon:** Dumb it down, keep it simple, and help people label you.

- **Practice, practice, practice...and then forget everything:** The key to a successful delivery is to do it naturally. With introductions, you also need to be able to tailor your delivery on the fly, depending on your audience and your call to action. Practice in front of the mirror, video yourself, and ask a friend to watch you. Do it again, and again, and again until you know every word by heart. Then forget the "speech" and get comfortable. Your ultimate goal is to connect authentically, in the moment, with your audience while still hitting all the high points of your brand.

- **Create multiple versions:** Your audience will change, your stage will change, and your call to action will change. Create different lengths and versions of your introduction so that you can easily and authentically give the appropriate introduction at the appropriate time.

- **Keep it simple:** People can't handle too many messages at one time. Keep your call to action to a single ask. You have a new program launching and want sign-ups? Don't ask for that *and* introductions. When you're aware of what's going on in your business and what your current objectives are, you can be purposeful and intentional about asking your audience for what you need.

- **Never apologize:** I've seen too many business owners stand up and start apologizing for not having a website or not being prepared. People aren't looking for perfect. They're looking for authentic. Never apologize for not having a website. Don't be contrite because your business card only has a name and email on it (more on this later). Own your awesomeness!

As I've said before, networking can be hard. For many of us, it's emotionally uncomfortable, and it pushes a lot of our buttons around being accepted and included. Add to that the need to be "on," to be articulate, to somehow sell ourselves without being salesy...it's a big mess. I know it must push at least a few of your buttons too. Otherwise, you wouldn't have chosen this book.

I may have gone from being someone who unapologetically hated networking to someone who's pretty good at it, but it's been a long journey—and one I'm still struggling with. Social anxiety is real, y'all!

But, I promised you that I'd show you ways to cultivate more confidence and build strategies and systems that take the sting out of networking. By helping you understand and define your brand and by showing you ways you can craft a simple but successful elevator speech, I hope I've taken some of the emotional sting out of your 30 to 60 seconds in the imaginary spotlight (and helped you fend off the lions in the process).

Listen, as with everything else in this book, I encourage you to take the bits that make the most sense to and for you and your business. Feel free to ignore the rest. The most important thing is your comfort level and your ability to be authentic in your networking activities. Because, friend, no one does *you* better than YOU.

Onward!

Prompts and Activities

- Download my Elevator Speech Worksheet at Lunchingwith-Lions.com, and use it to help you craft your compelling and engaging pitch.

- What are the emotional problems you solve for your clients?

- Get creative and think outside the box by creating a hook. Remember, it doesn't have to be funny! My "go to" hook is "I empower business owners to transform their business for greater revenue, greater control of their operations, and greater satisfaction." Not funny, but it grabs the audience's attention.

- What kind of social proof can you employ in your elevator speech?

- Based on your current goals and objectives, what will your elevator speech call to action be in the next 90 to 120 days?

NETWORKING FEARS

Time for a gut check.

The truth is that we can be all up in our business, understanding our objective, crystal clear on our goals. We can have our financial resources budgeted down to the last cent, and our calendar can be buttoned up like my grandpa's three-piece suit. Our elevator pitch can be absolutely pitch perfect. And we can still be afraid of networking.

It can still give us the willies.

It still gives me the willies from time to time (and, hey, I'm a Professional New Girl!).

Listen, unless we're psychopaths, we're all afraid of something at some time. Especially when we go outside our comfort zones and do something that challenges our primal selves (like meeting new people and joining the tribe). I'll proudly raise my hand and say that I, like many other people, suffer from that kind of fear when it comes to networking.

So, what do you do? You can have all the systems and strategies you want, but how do you take the leap when the net is nowhere in sight?

First, it can help to name the fear. What is it about networking that gives you the cold sweats? Let's talk about some of the most common fears and how you can work *within* them.

FEAR OF STRANGERS

When I was the new girl in class, I was afraid to make a move because I didn't know what the social rules were. Likewise, my new classmates were probably leery of me because (red alert!) I was a stranger to the group. The same basic fear of strangers can crop up when we network.

When you enter a networking group or event for the first time and feel that twinge of uncertainty or fear (big room, scary, not-friendly strangers) remind yourself that, most likely, there are plenty of other people there who don't know anyone either.

Work within your fear

There are some easy ways to work within this fear. Note that I don't say "overcome" your fear, because, frankly, I can't promise you ever will. I certainly still have fears that I face at every networking event and group I attend. But, having steps to follow and a system for working within your fear will take the emotional sting out of your experience and help you build that networking muscle. Over time, these steps and systems will become a habit, and eventually, your new normal.

- Look for people who are hanging back or sitting alone. Be the initiator by introducing yourself to them. You'll feel more confident when you take control, and they'll be thankful to you for reaching out (because, hey, they're probably freaked out too).

- Wear your name tag on your right shoulder so that, when you shake hands, it's clearly visible.[9] Your eye naturally travels down your own arm to the hand you're shaking, and up the right arm to the face of person you're greeting, landing smack dab on that name tag. If you wear your name tag on the left, people will see your face, but they'll have to search to figure out your name.

- If the event is seated, as at a luncheon, make it a point to introduce yourself to the people on either side of you and across the table.

- If the opportunity arises, volunteer to help—with anything. You'll get to meet everyone quickly if it's your job to hand out name tags or contact forms.

FEAR OF HAVING NOTHING TO SAY

Networking puts you on the spot. You're expected to stand up and deliver a soliloquy on your business (your elevator speech). You have to chit-chat with other people—strangers, even (gasp!)—for the duration of the event. And you can't be salesy, but you need to promote your business. You have to be authentic and witty and gracious and...geez. The pressure!

Many people genuinely fear the conversational part of networking. What if you stumble over your words? What if you blank out when someone asks you something about your business? What if you just flat run out of things to say?

Work within your fear

This one's easy.

Listen. Join a group and listen. Sit there, look pretty, and listen. Odds are, once the conversation gets going, you'll find openings for a question or two.

The key to making this work is to be an active listener. Face the speaker, and look that person in the eyes. Leave your phone on the table, or better yet, in your pocket or purse. Show that you're fully engaged in what the speaker is saying through your body language and by making small sounds of agreement. Ask relevant and pertinent questions when the opportunity arises.

By asking questions of the people you're meeting, not only do you take the pressure off yourself to carry the conversation, but you find natural and authentic ways to share information about yourself in response to what your conversation mates are saying.

When you show interest in other people by asking questions, they automatically start making deposits into your social currency account. Which just means they start to like you. And we all know the next stop on that train is trust!

FEAR OF LACK OF KNOWLEDGE OR LACK OF INTEREST

For me, this shows up when people ask me if I've heard of so-and-so, or if I listen to this or that podcast. The answer is usually no. See, I came to business coaching through the business side. I earned my knowledge in the trenches, so to speak, so I don't follow a lot of gurus or influencers. Sure, I have my own. *Entrepreneur Magazine* is my bible. Barbara Corcoran of *Shark Tank* is my idol. But, I don't spend a whole lot of time listening to podcasts and webinars (because I'm aware of what my business objectives are, so I'm purposeful about the trainings I engage in, and I'm intentional about how I spend my money and time).

Maybe for you, your lack of interest and knowledge shows up when people start talking about sports, or parenting, or politics. You know there's a topic out there that makes your eyes glaze over, and the thought that someone will ask you if you caught the latest cheese-rolling championship the other day causes you to huddle in fear. Yikes!

Work within your fear

Whatever it is, put those listening ears back on. In fact, this should be your default at most networking events until you feel more confident. Listening will get you everywhere. Because when someone is passionate about something, they love nothing more than an audience. (Professional New Girl Tip No. 83: Don't zone out while listening! Watch your resting bitch-face and remember to smile.)

And don't be afraid to out yourself. When someone asks me whether I heard a certain podcast or read a certain Facebook post by an influencer, I'll simply say, "No, I'm not familiar with that podcast. Can you tell me about it?" Question + Listen = Social Cred. Boom!

FEAR OF STANDING OUT—IN A BAD WAY

Every group has its own personality and customs. Some are dress-up events, some are "come as you are" (great for work-at-home entrepreneurs like me!). Some allow you to share events or programs with the group; others allow you to share, but you can't be too salesy (yes, I've run into that).

What if you wear the wrong thing?

What if you say the wrong thing?

What if you do it wrong?

What if you break the rules?

The lions are coming! The lions are coming!

As we've discussed, the fear of being outside the group—either because you didn't form the necessary connections or because you've done something to break the social contract—is a very real, very primal fear.

Work within your fear

This is one situation where I looooooooooove social media and the interwebs because it allows me to do a lot of research. You can too. Try some of the following:

- Look at pictures from past events for hints on what to wear or what to expect from the room setup. Will you be seated at large or small tables? Will you be standing? Is it a conference Room or a classroom-style setting?
- Check out the attendees list(s) to see who has attended events in the past and who is attending the event you're thinking of going to.
- If you have the time and the contact details, reach out to the facilitator with some basic questions. (This is great because it gives you an excuse to chat when you see that person at the event.)

If you can't suss out this kind of information before an event, take a look-and-listen approach to your first attendance to watch for cues and clues to the networking culture of the group.

And always overdress. (That's not a Professional New Girl Tip. That's a Dallas Girl tip!)

FEAR THAT YOU'LL SUCK AT NETWORKING

Yeah. This one I can claim. What if I just flat-out suck at networking? I show up wearing the wrong thing, my elevator speech sucks, people aren't interested in what I have to say, I forget my business cards, I embarrass myself by spilling my tea, I order the barbecue platter when everyone else orders salad, I offend someone with a poorly timed joke...I could go on and on. All the mind-junk comes up and brings its little gremlin fears out to play, and they can have a field day dreaming up ways I could blow it in a group or event.

Work within your fear

There's only one way I know through this fear, and it's the one I used. So, it's the one I'm encouraging you to try.

Practice.

Networking is like a muscle or a habit. You have to practice in order to get better and stronger at it. Remember that everyone is most likely experiencing fear on some level (unless they're psychopaths) and, just like you, are more concerned with themselves and how they're coping. They just assume *you're* doing great!

Practice meeting people by committing to talking to two or three strangers a day as you go about your life. They don't have to be long conversations. You can ask for a recommendation or directions, or chat about the weather, sports, or other local events. I find that chatting people up in the checkout line feels really natural. I'm stuck there, they're stuck there, and there's a *People* magazine with some salacious headline right in front of us that we can ogle over together. Perfect ingredients for a quick chat!

OTHER WAYS TO WORK WITHIN YOUR FEARS

Flip the script

This is what I call it when I work with my clients on affirmations. Affirmations can replace our negative thoughts (big room, scary, not-friendly strangers) with positive thoughts.

Affirmations aren't just for hippies, and they're not just for the crunchy granola crowd. MRI studies show that when we speak our affirmations aloud, the part of our brain responsible for forming new habits and behaviors lights up.[10] Spoken affirmations cause physiological changes in our brains. You can literally rewire your thoughts by speaking your positive mantras aloud.

For instance, if your networking fear centers around being the only new person in a group and other members not connecting with you, flip the script. Tell yourself, "Hey, if they've all been networking with each other for a while, they need some new blood. They'll be excited to meet me and make a new connection!"

Create an affirmation for yourself that's the *opposite* of your fear.

Here's an exercise I give to my clients. Take a sheet of paper, and draw a vertical line down the middle. On the left side of the paper, write the heading "Fears," and on the right side, write "Affirmations." Now, start writing down all the fears you have about networking. Don't filter your thoughts. This isn't for anyone but you to read. Get real with yourself and be honest. What do you fear? What's holding you back from being the networking dynamo I know you can be? Brain dump it all right there onto that paper.

FEAR		AFFIRMATION
There's already a sloth herder in this group, so no one will be interested in me.	➤➤	I have something of unique value to offer this group.
Other professional women intimidate me.	➤➤	People see me as an expert in my field.
They'll think I'm stupid.	➤➤	People see me as someone they admire.

Once you've got all that mindjunk out and listed on the page, head over to the right-hand side of the paper. For each fear, create an affirmative statement that is its opposite. Here's an example:

Here are some of the other affirmations I like:

- I find it easy to network with others.
- I am well connected.
- It's natural and easy for me to get along with other people.
- I'm always asking people for their contact information.
- My networking skills are top-notch.
- Being social is my natural way of life.
- People see me as someone who knows people.
- The people I network with enjoy talking to me.

What are your fears? How can you flip the script?

Act "as if"

We hear it all the time: you have to "fake it 'til you make it." This is why I encourage the networking-averse to create systems and strategies for networking. They give you a process to follow, steps to complete, and when you repeat them over and over, they eventually become natural.

Years and years ago, I was in therapy. The therapist suggested I should basically fake it until I made it, in terms of getting back on my emotional feet. She shared this great story to illustrate her point, and I'm going to share it with you. So, quickly, run and get some popcorn. I'll wait.

Once upon a time, there was a criminal who was so well known for his crimes that he couldn't leave his home and move freely about in society. So, he devised a plan. He crafted a mask that showed the face of a saint. He would don the mask and leave home, free to move about the markets and streets without being noticed.

The man quickly realized, however, that in order to pull off the ruse of being a saint, he could no longer engage in criminal activities. He not only had to wear the face of the saint, but he also had to affect the behaviors and demeanor of a saint in order to be believable.

Years went by, and the man continued to go out wearing the mask and behaving like a saint. Until, one day, he realized he could no longer remove the mask. He had become the saint. What had started off as a deception had become his truth.

Isn't that a great story? I still think of it all the time. Because being a business owner is hard, and I know I don't always feel like I'm good enough or smart enough to be doing what I do—and getting paid for it. Sometimes, I just have to fake it until I make it in terms of pricing my services, having a sales conversation, or networking.

I'm going to tell you a little secret. I have an alter ego! Shhhhh! She's not a superhero or anything. It's not a Clark Kent/Superman thing. It's more like a blonde-ponytail-and-twinset-goody-two-shoes Sandy at the drive-in/teased-hair-red-lipstick-black-leather-pants Sandy at the carnival thing. My alter ego's name is KP.

KP is awesome. KP is a master networker and an entrepreneurial genius! She always looks put together. She knows a ton of people. She's super confident and never gets nervous in social situations.

KP is a badass.

Because she's not real. I'm Katherine, and I'm a hot mess. And, I do mean it. A. Hot. Mess. But, remember in *The Wizard of Oz*, when the Wizard shouts, "Pay no attention to the man behind the curtain!"? KP is the Wizard. Me? I'm hanging out behind the curtain.

When I'm facing my networking fears, I sometimes think "WWKPD?" (what would KP do?). Then I do that. I feel like I'm playing a part, but it's a part that helps me achieve my objectives.

KP walks right up to that stranger (big room, scary, not friendly), sticks out her hand, and asks for a coffee date. KP sails into networking events where she doesn't know a soul. KP prices her proposals waaaaay over what I'd be comfortable asking for (and she usually gets it). And, guess what. KP takes me and my business right along with her. Her success is ultimately my success.

Earlier, I talked about the Law of Attraction and how it helps us manifest our desires. One of the ways it works is by helping us focus on how we want to feel. Whether it's by choosing a word that we repeat to ourselves, or creating a vision board we can look at, or engaging in visualization exercises, when we focus on how we want to feel, we consciously and subconsciously begin to align our activities in ways that help us get there.

When I suggest creating an alter ego, I'm not encouraging you to be inauthentic or fake. In fact, I'm hoping my suggestion will help you become *more* authentic. When I suggest that you act "as if," I'm applying the Law of Attraction to help you imagine how you *want* to feel when you're networking and then aligning your actions to feel like that for real. Imagine what would change and how you'd feel if you acted:

- *As if* you were comfortable introducing yourself to strangers
- *As if* you had all the confidence in the world and no fears about what to say
- *As if* you were incredibly engaging and charismatic
- *As if* you rocked at networking

When you act "as if," you put your fears at arm's length and give yourself some breathing room. Inside that space, you can create the habits and build the muscles that will, eventually, make acting "as if" unnecessary. You will, eventually, become the saint. Or, in this case, the master networker.

Ground yourself

Usually, when I roll up to a networking event, I've been on the hamster wheel all day. Up early, teens out the door, calls, client work, and then I'm rushing across town to an event where I have to be "on"—engaging, charming, and authentic. By the time I pull into a parking lot, I'm generally pretty frazzled. And it's hard to switch from frazzled to "on" in the 150 feet between my parking space and the door.

That's why I like to stop, sit quietly, and use conscious breathing to calm and focus myself before every networking event.

Let me explain.

Right before I get out of my car to head inside, I take a moment to do some deep breathing and to focus on my intention. I turn off the ignition, turn on my white-noise app (there are lots of guided meditation apps you can find if you want something a little more structured), and close my eyes.

Keep in mind, my intention ties directly to my business objectives (awareness) and my reasons for being at that particular event (purpose).

Part of the exercise is doing a mindfulness scan of how I'm feeling right now, in this moment, as I sit in my car. Am I stressed? How is my breathing? Am I thinking about a late project? Am I coming from a fun lunch with friends? Where am I, physically and emotionally?

I ask myself to affirm my purpose for being at this event, and both the immediate and long-term results I want to achieve. With whom do I want to connect? What are my goals? How will today's event further my business success?

When I'm focusing my intention, I choose two to three words that describe how I want to feel and be while networking. Is my intention today to be "open" and "calm"? Or is it to be "strong" and "direct"?

Once I know how I want to feel and be, I engage in 4-4-8 breathing. I breathe deep into my belly for four counts, hold it for four counts, and release it slowly for eight counts. A hypnotherapist friend taught me this sequence, and explained that the 4-4-8 breathing technique helps dissipate adrenaline in your system. Adrenaline is the stress hormone that causes rapid breathing and heartbeat. It's the sizzle in the frazzle. Not something you want around if you're trying to calm and ground yourself.

As I breathe, I repeat to myself the words I've chosen: "I am calm. I am open." Usually, I try to spend at least five minutes breathing and repeating my words before I slowly come back to the outside world and allow myself to get out of the car.

Try this the next time you arrive at an event stressed and nervous. Ask yourself how you want to feel and be during the event and in your interactions with other members. Breathe deep and ground yourself.

Power pose

Speaking of adrenaline, did you know you can trick your body into thinking that you're calm, confident, and comfortable? Yep. You can do it with Power Poses.

When we humans feel afraid or insecure, we tend to draw into ourselves. Hunching our shoulders, crossing our arms, minimizing big movements—we try to make ourselves smaller.

But when we feel good and strong, we expand. Think about runners crossing the finish line—arms thrown up, head thrown back, the ecstasy of victory on their faces.

It turns out that certain body postures not only reflect how we feel in the moment (winning the race), but they can also significantly influence us to change our mental and physical state to bring about the same feeling of power. Power Poses.

The first Power Pose is often called the "Wonder Woman" pose. Stand straight, feet firmly planted a little more than hip-width apart. Make fists with your hands and place them on your hips. Shoulders back, chest open.

The second is the "Boss Man" pose (at least, that's what I call it). When you're sitting at your desk, lean back in your chair. Place your feet on your desk with ankles crossed. Raise your arms and put your hands behind your head.

Hold either pose for two minutes.

Right about now, you're probably wondering how on Earth these goofy poses could possibly trick your body into thinking that everything's cool.

Well, let me tell you!

Turns out, when you engage in a Power Pose for at least two minutes, your body releases more testosterone and less cortisol.[11] Testosterone is found in both men and women, and it's the hormone related to libido and strength. Cortisol, however, is a hormone related to stress. More testosterone can mean more energy and confidence. In fact, men with low testosterone frequently report being shy and lacking confidence. Less cortisol means a greater sense of calm. In other words, maintaining a Power Pose for two minutes can help you feel calmer and more confident.

The next time you feel the sizzle in your frazzle start to flare up, spend a couple of minutes channeling Linda Carter in her little American-flag onesie, gold bracelets, and golden lasso. You're Wonder Woman—or the Big Boss Man (no gender discrimination here)!

Power on!

Am I convincing you yet that your fears around networking are unfounded? I know, I know. In your mind, they seem totally real and reasonable. But take a closer look.

Here's a quick dose of reality:

- People are not, on balance, vindictive or deliberately hurtful.
- Most people want others to succeed and be happy, and they're prepared to help you.
- People will overlook your shyness, forgive a couple of stumbles and stutters, and treat you with compassion.

If all the science and quackery I just shared isn't enough, here's a little pep talk from Stuart Smalley of Saturday Night Live: "You're good enough, you're smart enough, and doggonit, people like you!"[12]

Prompts and Activities

- Grab a piece of paper and write down how you're feeling. Then set a timer and try the Wonder Woman or Boss Man pose. When you're done, take a second piece of paper and write down how you feel. Compare the two. Do you feel calmer and more uplifted?

- What's the root fear you face when you're networking?

- How do you want to feel when you engage in networking?

- What affirmations or mantras can you create for yourself to counteract that fear?

- In what ways would acting "as if" help you feel more in control of your fears?

HELLO
my name is

Chapter 14

ONLINE NETWORKING

If you're like most entrepreneurs, you're happy to while away your days dreaming up new products and fantasizing about your extraordinary success. Personally, I love the five-second commute from my kitchen to my home office and the ability to work in my pajamas all day.

Which is why online networking rocks.

Well, okay. That's only part of the reason why online networking is so awesome. Here are some of the other reasons I like it:

It's easy.

It's fast.

It's free.

For the networking-averse, online connecting can be a godsend because it literally puts distance between you and other humans. It removes some of the social pressures and fears we've talked about throughout this book.

Online networking also allows us to associate with people we might not otherwise ever meet. When you engage online, you can connect with people from all over the world. Whether you're looking for thought partners or industry connections, online net-working immediately opens you up to new perspectives and ideas on how to run your business. It can also help expose your brand to an infinite number of potential clients if you're purposeful and intentional about where you spend your time online.

As I mentioned earlier, the fast, easy, and free nature of online networking can also have a negative side. It can be much harder to ask for introductions, make connections, and build those crucial and authentic relationships precisely because of that comfortable physical distance.

Online networking creates physical distance that can make it harder to build authentic relationships.

Connecting with someone online is great. It's direct and to the point, and you can get right to the nut of what you want that connec-tion to result in. What it doesn't do is easily allow for the personal in-teraction that relationships are built on. It doesn't allow for the "get to know you" chit-chat that forms the first two legs of that all-important "know, like, trust" foundation of an authentic connection.

If you've been engaging professionally online, or if you're just dipping your toe into the networking waters of the World Wide Web, it helps to have a plan.

First, let's define what we're talking about. Online network-ing is any engagement with other humans that takes place mainly on the interwebs—primarily on dedicated networking platforms such as LinkedIn and social media channels such as Facebook, Instagram, and Twitter. There are also groups for various interests and industries on sites such as Reddit, and private forums and discussion groups on niche sites such as Engineerboards.com. And, don't overlook the comment sections on the blogs and articles of your favorite special-interest or industry influencers. (Note: when I use the word "industry," I'm speaking about your industry as well as the industry of your ideal client.)

Understanding who is using various platforms (awareness) will help you find the right channel for your objectives. As of this writing, LinkedIn is still the top B2B channel. Previously, Facebook was considered a B2C channel, but more recently, Facebook and Twitter have consistently topped the list of preferred channels for marketers overall. (I always recommend that my clients maintain a presence on Facebook, regardless of whether they're B2B or B2C, because nearly one out of five people on the planet are on Facebook). If your targets are super-nichey, it might require some research to find the best place to engage. You can Google "[Insert Industry] forum" to help locate special-interest groups. You can also ask your clients where they're connecting online.

The more targeted you can be about where you're engaging, the more likely your target will hear your message. What do I mean? With 1.32 billion daily active users on Facebook,[13] that platform can be noisy. Add to that the constant changes Mr. Zuckerberg and his team are making to the algorithms regarding what business content is and isn't seen, and it can be easy for a small business with a limited budget of time and money to get lost in the crowd.

On the other hand, if you're engaging in a niche group on Reddit or an industry-specific group such as Engineerboards.com, the number of users is infinitely smaller. Which means that each voice within the group is more noticeable. Add to that a voice that contributes valuable content (more on this later), and you're much more likely to get noticed by your targets in a positive way.

As with everything in this book, I want you to be aware of your reason for networking online, purposeful about finding the right channels for your efforts, and intentional about your engagement on those channels. Even though online networking is fast, it still requires a constant presence in order to be truly effective and get the results you want. Understanding your time availability will help you narrow down the best platforms for achieving your objectives. The primary resource expenditure when networking online is time, so ask yourself:

- How much time do I have available each day to engage with my online network?
- How much time am I willing to spend engaging online each day?

I ask about willingness because we can spend hours, literally, getting lost in social media. We're reading a relevant blog article and...oh, look, Bob got a new puppy! When I work with clients to develop their social media plan, I ask them to dedicate time each day and to have a plan for how that time will be spent. For instance:

LinkedIn (30 minutes daily)
- Review/make connection requests (5 minutes)
- Check messages and respond (5 minutes)
- Post update (3 minutes, 3x per week)
- Research targets (10 minutes)
- Engage on feed and in special interest groups (likes, comments, shares: 7 minutes)

Facebook (30 minutes daily)
- Post update (5 minutes)

- Research targets/engage in their feeds (likes, comments, shares: 15 minutes)
- Engage in special interest groups (likes, comments, shares: 10 minutes)

Focus, people, focus! That's an hour of engagement each day on just two channels.

"Wait a minute," I can hear you saying. "You said online networking was *fast*. An hour a day or more doesn't seem very fast!"

Yes, you're right. An hour a day does seem like a lot. So, let's put it into perspective.

If you were to attend a one-hour networking event, you'd spend an hour at the event itself, plus travel time to and from. For argument's sake, let's say it took 20 minutes for you to drive to the event. That's an hour and 40 minutes. There were 30 people at the event who heard your elevator speech, and during the event, you got to speak with four of them individually. You left with a coffee date with one of those four people.

Now, let's compare that time to networking online.

You set aside an hour to engage online. That's an hour (time saved: 40 minutes).

Let's look at what you achieved during just your 30 minutes on LinkedIn. The average LinkedIn user has between 500 and 999 connections (we'll use the low end for our purposes).[14] During the half hour on LinkedIn, you shared a post that will be seen by your 500 connections, so now they all know what's going on with you and your business (Professional New Girl Tip No. 53: this is a great place to use social proof to show that working with you is the correct behavior). You accepted three new connections, and you corresponded individually with five people through messaging. You then engaged in your special groups, which have a total of 5,000 members.

Quick math says that potentially 5,500 people saw your name and associated (valuable) content and comments with your brand during those 30 minutes. If we use the 80/20 rule to be conservative, that means that 1,100 people probably really saw it and digested it. You also got more up-close and personal with the eight people with whom you connected and messaged. Let's assume, also for argument's sake, that one of those messages you received was a request for a one-hour introductory call.

To compare:

In-person engagement: 1 hour 40 minutes = exposure to 30 people
Online engagement: 30 minutes = exposure to 1,100 people

Now, do it all again tomorrow...and we're up to 2,200 people on *LinkedIn alone*. Sure, some of them are the same people who saw you today, but that's okay. Heck, that's great—because you got to put yourself in front of them twice with valuable, relevant content and comments. Every time they see your brand and associate it with interesting insights into the ongoing discussion, you grow your credibility and expertise, and you build trust.

I'm not recommending that you forgo all in-person networking activities in favor of online networking. What I'm suggesting is that when you define your objectives and build your networking plan, be aware of the potential results of networking online and intentional about how you do it. In-person and online networking both have a place in your plan, so don't put all those proverbial eggs in one basket.

Prompts and Activities

How do you identify the right online platforms on which to engage? Ask yourself:

- What are my objectives for networking online (professional development, strategic partnerships, resources for my own business, lead generation, new clients, etc.)?

- Who is my ideal target? Am I looking to connect with people in my own industry? In industries that can support my business? Or am I aiming for my ideal client?

- Which platform is my ideal target using?

- In which online groups is my ideal target engaging?

TAKE IT OFF-LINE

I like to say that social media is like a cocktail party. You wouldn't show up at your friend Bob's house, jump up on the coffee table, and start shouting about your business. The same goes for engaging online. You want to be part of the conversation, asking questions and chiming in when you have relevant and helpful information. There's a time and a place for a sales pitch, but just like when you're networking in person, the people you're engaging with online will give you signals when they're ready to engage in a sales conversation.

When you're online every day, engaging in the discussion, people will start to notice you and what you're offering. Likewise, you should start to recognize the names of other regular contributors. The first thing to do is to really pay attention to what people are asking and posting on the conversation threads (pssst...think of this as listening at an in-person networking event).

For instance, I participate in several local moms' networking groups on Facebook. When the question falls under my expertise (entrepreneurship and running your own business), I'll make suggestions or offer resources. I won't be salesy, but I'll say things like, "I'm a small business strategist, and I often recommend that my clients..." or "As a business strategist, I find my clients really benefit from [Insert Resource]." I'm tuned into the original poster's comment or question, and I'm also paying attention to what other commenters are saying. So, I'll respond to both the original post and reply to other comments as appropriate.

As. Appropriate.

Remember, the goal here is to show up, be authentic, and offer valuable, relevant content in order to grow those "know, like, and trust" factors.

- When you show up regularly, other users get to know you.
- When you contribute entertaining, informational, and pertinent content that they can use, they begin to like you.
- When you do so in an authentic, generous way with no expectation of making a sale, they begin trust you.

Eventually, you'll start to identify targets from these types of engagements. Whether it's a professional connection on LinkedIn or another mom in a moms' group on Facebook, it's entirely fitting for you to reach out to them directly to ask for a connection.

This is one place where I really, really want you to be intentional. Because the moment you start making overtures to a stranger to build a connection digitally, you edge over into the same type of relationship-building that you do in person. The time commitment increases, and the need to build rapport through interpersonal interaction increases. Sure, you can half-ass it and add a bunch of semifamiliar names to your contacts on LinkedIn or your friends on Facebook, but why would you?

What I've come to realize since I completed my personal networking challenge is that networking is a constant balancing of quality versus quantity: how many people you want to add to your network versus what types of relationships you want to have. Awareness is key, not only in your business but also with yourself.

How much energy do you have to invest in these new relationships (and still love up on your family and friends)?

How much do you *want* to invest?

CONNECT

Remember, there's no right or wrong answer here—only the right answer for you and your business. Maybe you need a tight group of strategic partners to funnel business your way and offer complimentary services. Or, maybe you need exposure to thousands of people (but not necessarily be on a first name basis with all of them) in order to grow your brand. Again, being aware of your objectives and goals along with being purposeful about making the right connections with the right people will help you achieve your intent.

When you're sure that an online connection is one that you want to grow, you'll need to reach out to them not once, but twice. First, you'll want to make a request for a connection.

Perhaps you've received a connection request on LinkedIn that looks something like this:

"Hi, [Insert Name]. I see we have quite a few connections in common, and I'd like to add you to my professional network."

Or, I've recently been getting this one:

"As an industry leader, I'd like to add you to my professional network."

(Stop! I'm blushing!)

There was a time in its early inception that LinkedIn recommended only connecting with people you knew. While LinkedIn itself still recommends guarding your connections, it seems that the custom has loosened quite a bit, and people today are linking left and right on the platform. Again, it's entirely up to you which and how many people you connect with, but I encourage you to be aware of your goals and be purposeful about who those people are (tired of me yet?).

Because people are connecting more frequently with strangers online, those who are aware and purposeful about their connections need more than the generic "please add me" request. You have 300 characters available to you in your connection invitation message. Use them to your advantage:

- If you're connecting with someone you know, it's a great opportunity to build on your existing relationship by saying something nice.

- If you're connecting with someone you don't know well, remind them of where you met or of which contacts you have in common to create an affiliation.

- If you're connecting with someone you don't know at all, this could be your only opportunity to establish a relationship with them. Use all the weapons at your disposal to wow them and stand out from the other requests they get every day.

So, what does that look like?

Connecting with a colleague:

"Hi, [Insert Name]. I really enjoyed working with you recently on the Jones's project and appreciated your contributions on the Yearly Widget Forecast. I'm looking forward to more chances to work together soon."

Connecting with a former coworker:

"Hi, [Insert Name. Congratulations on the job move to Widgets R Us. I was recently reminded of our time together at Widget House from 2002 to 2010 and how much I learned from you about Widget forecasting. I'd love to catch up and learn more about your new position."

Connecting with someone you just met:

"Hi, [Insert Name]. It was lovely to meet you today at the Widget Foundation luncheon. I was really intrigued by the work you're doing with the Future Widget Makers of America. I'd love to connect to learn more."

Connecting with a stranger:

"Hi, [Insert Name]. I was recently speaking with Bob Jones, and he shared your business with me. After reading your treatise on the History of Widget Worship in America, I'd love to connect. If you ever have 20 minutes or so, I'd love to hear about how you've leveraged your Widget expertise and what skills you think are relevant to someone who'd like to do the same."

Connecting with someone in the same LinkedIn Group:

"Hi, [Insert Name]. I'm also in the Society of Professional Widget Manufacturers, and I've really enjoyed reading your posts. The article you shared last week about custom widget design was pretty thought-provoking. I'd love to stay in touch and learn more about your work."

I could go on, but what I'd like to point out is that each request for connection has a few things in common:

- **It shows interest in the other person.** Take a few minutes to check out your target's profile and note the information that genuinely interests you. Reference a conversation you've had with your target or mention a shared interest. People like being noticed. It flatters them and instantly creates a positive attitude toward you and an affinity for your request.
- **It establishes an existing connection.** Demonstrating even the slightest connection between you and your target is social proof ("see, we already know/like/trust the same things!"). Whether that connection is direct, as in the case of a former colleague, or more of a stretch, as with a stranger, taking the time to illustrate what connects you with your target will build a sense of like-mindedness and make that person more open to accepting your request.
- **It explains why you want to connect.** People are leery of random generic connection requests because those are the ones that generally start spamming us with sales messaging after we accept them (in my experience). Be specific about

why you want to connect with your target to eliminate any distrust and set the intention for the relationship you hope to have.

Facebook doesn't have an automatic mechanism for messaging your targets when you make a friend request. You can send them a message separately through Facebook Messenger, and I suggest you do that. Especially if you're connecting with strangers for business purposes.

A note on Facebook and business connections. Since I started working primarily with women business owners, I've found that I receive a lot of friend requests on Facebook from women I've met through networking. However, I've never received a friend request from a male business owner after a networking event.

I have a Facebook business page, and I have a presence on LinkedIn, and yet women want to connect on my personal Facebook page. This is a tricky situation. On the one hand, I post private information and share pictures and details about my kids, family, and political views on my personal page, and I don't necessarily want either (1) professional contacts or (2) strangers to be privy to that content. On the other hand, I don't want to shut down someone who wants to build a deeper connection.

Women, in particular, tend to blur the lines between the professional and the personal, which can detract from them being viewed as experts. When we act in a less than professional way (i.e., when we *don't* look like we have our sh*t together), we undermine our authority and our value. How people perceive us is directly reflected in how much they're willing to pay for our service and how much they respect and rate what we have to offer. Too many of my clients come to me lamenting the fact that they're not attracting the types of clients who are willing to pay a premium for what they have to sell. Frequently, when I examine their brand, I discover that the way they're presenting themselves in the world doesn't align with the vision they have for themselves and their business. They're perceived as less knowledgeable and less professional, because of the way they interact online and in person.

We build the perception of our brand and our worth with everything we do in business, and I encourage women business owners to elevate their online connections by positioning themselves and their businesses as professional. If you're connecting with someone you've met through business, such as on their business page on Facebook, follow their business page on Twitter and Instagram, and connect with them on LinkedIn. Spend time growing your in-person relationship before you shift your connections from professional to personal by friending them on Facebook.

My approach to accepting Facebook friend requests from professional contacts is two-pronged:

- I tag all professional contacts as "Acquaintances" so that I can filter them out of the most private posts.
- Every six months or so, I clean up my Friends list by creating a post that says, "I am cleaning up my Friends list to include only personal connections. If we know each other primarily through our businesses, please like my business page or connect with me on LinkedIn, and I will do the same."

Okay, stepping off the soapbox now (and, hey, if you want to connect with me online, check out my LinkedIn profile or like my business page on Facebook).

I recommended earlier that in order to make a solid connection online, you'll want to reach out to your target not once, but twice. The first ask is for the connection itself, which we just reviewed. The second ask is to take the online connection off-line.

Before you do that, though, you're going to want to schmooze your contact a bit. Create some familiarity and goodwill so that they're receptive when they get the request from you to invest time in building a deeper connection. This is where the online engagement comes in and where your daily plan for that engagement starts to pay off.

LIKE

Come on, admit it. You peek at who's given you a thumbs up on your posts, don't you? I'm going to bet your targets do too (at least some of the time). When you're scrolling through your feed, click on that Like button to let people know you're paying attention.

COMMENT

Because we're notified of comments on our posts, a few remarks on the content your targets have shared will definitely grab their attention. We all like to be appreciated and know that what we're sharing is delivering value, so your comments will be welcomed. LinkedIn will also notify you of job changes, promotions, and anniversaries, so email your targets words of congratulations to recognize the occasion. As with your connection request, don't send the standard blurb provided by LinkedIn. Take a minute to personalize it. This personal touch can lead to deeper conversations.

SHARE

Share the content posted by your targets. Doing so says you think they're experts and have offered something other people need to see. Especially if they wrote and posted it themselves! On the flip side, once you've studied your targets' profiles, share articles, books, and resources with them that they may find helpful or interesting.

MEETING IRL

Now that you've made the connection and grown your "know, like, and trust" factor by engaging online, it's time to move your virtual connection off-line and meet IRL (in real life).

This can be the scary part, just like any networking situation. Until now, you've been relatively anonymous, connecting from your pajamas at your computer. Engaging in cyberspace and enjoying the physical space that it gave you. Now, though, you're going to have to start taking some risks to move your relationship from the anonymity of the interwebs, to the much more personal and vulnerable in-person interaction.

Online connections can only go so far. Eventually, you're going to want to take some, or most of them, off-line (especially if you've been purposeful and intentional with creating connections to people who will help you reach your objectives). The delightful thing about connecting and engaging online, as we've been discussing, is that it really lowers social barriers once you meet in person. After all, you've been joining in an online conversation, sharing content, commenting on posts of similar interest, asking questions, and congratulating each other. Gosh, it's like you almost already know the person by the time you meet face-to-face (insert sarcasm font).

But how do you get face-to-face?

1. **Are you attending a conference or business event?**
   Whether the event is local or out of town, let your network
   know. Invite people to connect with you at the event for
   coffee or a meal.

2. **Watch your connections' feeds.** Are they traveling to a
   conference or seminar in or near your town? Have they
   RSVP'd to a local business happening? If so, reach out and
   arrange to meet them while they're in your neck of the
   woods, or connect with them at the event.

3. **Attend off-line meetings with online groups.** The same
   organizations that sponsor those niche forums and special interest groups on LinkedIn and Facebook often hold
   off-line meetings. People usually find and participate in
   WEBO Network through our social media groups before
   attending an in-person event. You can do the same! Make
   it a point to visit an event and connect with the people
   with whom you've been engaging online.

4. **Call them.** Yep, you knew I'd get here eventually. Pick up
   the phone and call them. Or, if that's too scary for you,
   email them and request to schedule a phone chat. Arrange
   a video call, or meet in person for coffee.

Whichever way you decide to connect with your virtual business buddies IRL, use the same three points you used in your request for a connection: show interest in them, remind them of
your connection, and be specific about why you want to connect
in person. Never use the term "I want to pick your brain" (ew!).
Be specific. Tell them you want to learn more about their journey

to their current position, or about what skills they recommend that you learn, or about how to connect to someone they know. Remember that when you're reaching out to them, you're setting the intention for your meeting, so take the opportunity to define that interaction.

If you've been engaging online with your target in the right ways, they'll know you've been following them. Which means this is not a casual, one-off invitation. They'll recognize (if they've been paying attention) that you've been following them, engaging with them—and showing long-term, sustained interest. And now you want to take it to the next level.

So, when you meet for that coffee, or that lunch, or that video chat—or whatever it is you decide to do in terms of face-to-face engagement—they're going to be open to creating a relationship with you because you've already been schmoozing them. You've wooed them by engaging with them online.

This might be a good time for me to jump in and remind you that networking is a long game, so none of this is going to happen overnight. Don't expect to connect with someone online, engage with them for a few days, and immediately enjoy a solid relationship that you can rely on for business and referrals. It could take weeks and even months before you're ready to take the next step in moving your relationship off-line, if that's your goal.

Networking is part of your overall marketing and business plan. It's just one arm in a multipronged approach to growing your brand presence, forming partnerships, and developing leads. Likewise, online marketing is only part of your networking plan. It should support and work with your in-person efforts.

If it all seems overwhelming, remember the best way to eat an elephant. What? You don't know? The best way to eat an elephant is one bite at a time. So, relax. Take a bite out of your networking plan today, then take another bite tomorrow, until you've eaten the whole damn pachyderm and built a kick-ass network in the process.

Prompts and Activities

- Create a daily plan for online engagement.

- Join groups that align with your goals and objectives (LinkedIn, Facebook).

- With whom do you need to be connecting online to further your goals and objectives? Create a target list of dream connections and start stalking them!

TRACKING YOUR RESULTS

How's your booty doing? I only ask because, as I've said before, I frequently hear business owners lament that they've been networking their booty off and not getting results. I want to make sure your booty is hanging in there as you build a solid networking practice.

Here's the thing about networking: the results aren't always apparent right away. Networking is a long game. It's an investment in long-term relationships that will support your business goals. It takes time for people to know, like, *and* trust you. The people you meet aren't running back to their offices to make a list of all the ways you can work together, or immediately emailing their own networks with referrals. In fact, even if they're super impressed with you and what you offer, they might not have an opportunity to work with you or even recommend you for months.

It's because of this that networking results can sometimes seem vague. After all, if you go to an event, meet someone with whom you click professionally, have a great connection and obvious opportunities to work together, and then...(crickets)...is it *really* working? It can be disheartening to spend the kind of time we've talked about and not have a tangible result right away.

It really can seem as though you're networking your booty off with no results to show for it. That's why tracking your efforts and outcomes is important to keep you motivated.

This is probably a good place to reiterate that *networking is not sales.* If it were, it would be so much easier to track! You make so many cold calls and close so many sales, and voila! You have an ROI! Or, if you run a Facebook ad for a program, you can measure your ad spend against enrollment to calculate a hard number result.

One of the best analogies I've heard about networking is from Dr. Ivan Misner, founder of BNI. He said networking is like an orchard. When you plant a single seed, you don't expect anything the first year, or the second, or probably even the third. But give it time and nurture, and by the fourth year, you'll be enjoying the proverbial fruits of your labor. That single seed multiplies and becomes a whole grove of apple trees.[15]

Although the results of networking probably won't take years, they do take time. Most people I know get an early boost in their business just by showing up and being the new kid. But the real growth and results come after you've taken time to grow a solid professional network. Your orchard. That's when your contacts start referring you to their own networks, and you begin to get calls from people who are connected to you through several channels. Remember the client who was recommended to me by the doctor *I'd never even met?* It happens. When you take the time to build your network, business will come to you from so many directions and so many sources that you may not even be able to identify which branch of your network is responsible.

All because you planted a seed and nurtured it into a network of fruitful connections.

Remember the survey in which business owners who credited networking for some or most of their success were dedicating 6.3 hours a week to networking activities? The same survey showed that those business owners who were enjoying the most success also tracked their results and monetary gains from networking. Those business owners who said that networking played no role in their success? They had no system for tracking their results.

Just sayin'.

The people who are networking and who have implemented systems to track their results are the ones who are getting the most business. The saying "what we pay attention to grows" is really relevant when it comes to networking. The more aware of our objectives, purposeful in our activities, and intentional in tracking and understanding the results we are, the more productive and successful we can be.

Tracking outcomes doesn't have to be a big, elaborate process. In fact, I suggest you start by focusing on the following five areas:

- Your contacts
- The organizations and events you're participating in and the results you're getting from them
- The amount of time and money you're investing in networking activities
- The amount of money you're making from networking and referrals, as well as the percentage this amount is of your business
- Systems for following up and staying in touch with the people you've met

There are dedicated business networking apps and customer relationship managers (CRMs) and a gazillion other special software tools and platforms you can use to track your contacts, results, and follow-up systems. Some simply organize your data, and some will automatically trigger activities (such as follow-ups) with calendar reminders. When you're just starting out, it can be overwhelming to audit, review, and select the right system for your needs—especially before you even know what your needs really are.

My recommendation is that you start your documentation with a good, old-fashioned spreadsheet. This allows you to adapt what and how you're tracking until you develop the processes and routines that work for you. Once you know how you like to record and manage your information, you'll be better positioned to invest in a more robust system or platform, if that's your goal.

ORGANIZING YOUR CONTACTS

Simply put, you gotta know who you know. As I write this, I have three stacks of business cards on my desk. Each stack contains at least 50 cards. And these cards are just from *this month's* networking activities! If I didn't have a way to organize these contacts for future reference, these little slips of paper would just be fodder for my recycling bin.

When I'm networking, I'm not only trying to connect with potential clients. I'm also connecting with:

- Collaborators with whom I might want to partner
- Contractors I can tap into when I need a certain service or product
- Connectors who can provide referrals
- Cool kids I just want to add to my tribe

I need a way to systematize those names and relationships so that I can easily and quickly find a contact—for example, if I want to offer a client a specific resource to help them succeed in their goals, if I need to outsource some project work, or if my computer goes kaput and I need a local service provider.

When I organize my contacts, I note:

- Contact name
- Business name
- Industry
- Email
- Phone number
- Physical address
- Where/how I met them (through an organization, an event, a referral, etc.)
- Type of contact (one of the Five Cs – Connector, Collaborator, Contractor, Client, or Cool Kid)
- Date of last contact
- Months since last contact or until next contact (I use both, depending on whether it's someone with whom I want to maintain regular contact, such as a power partner, or someone with whom I want to touch base at regular intervals, but there's no compelling reason to schedule a next contact)
- Notes

Some of these categories are self-explanatory, but let me explain the others.

Classifying information into general industry categories allows me to search for certain contact characteristics. For example, if I'm looking to outsource some content development, I can search my database for all the copywriters and then reach out to them individually for proposals. Likewise, if I'm recommending web design to a client, I can pull names in that industry fairly easily and offer them up. Cross-referencing contacts who fall into one of the Five Cs with their industry allows me to drill down even more on what they have to offer.

Typically, my order of priority for maintaining contact with a connection is (1) client, (2) connector, and (3) collaborator. Tracking the last date of contact and how long it's been since I connected with someone is the basis of my follow-up system. I want to maintain regular contact with clients and connectors so that I stay top of mind, as well as with collaborators because we're power partners for each other's businesses and we need to be in regular communication. Generally, I'll set a specific date for the next contact with these connections, either together with them or on my own calendar for follow-up.

Cool kids, contractors, and some less advantageous connectors and collaborators don't require nurturing as frequently. By tracking the months since my last contact with them, I can keep the length between connections in check and reach out when my schedule allows.

Just a reminder: a connection or contact can be any type of personal engagement (in other words, drip campaigns to your email list don't count). You can engage with people via a personal email, a note sent by snail mail, a phone call, a video call, connecting with them at a networking event, or scheduling an in-person meeting. These are intentional connections with individual contacts for specific reasons related to your objectives and goals.

I use the "Notes" section of my contact organizer to record reminders about our conversations, items I promised to follow up with, referrals I promised to make, etc. This is a good way to remind myself about upcoming events in my contact's business so that I can recognize their successes and follow up in an authentic way. It's also a great way to organize my follow-ups for referrals and new business (i.e., thank-you gifties).

Visit LunchingwithLions.com to find some ideas for how to organize your contact spreadsheet.

ORGANIZATIONS AND EVENTS

We've spent a lot of time talking about the different types of organizations in which you can network, how to choose the right groups for you and your goals, and how to calculate the ROI on your time and financial investment for participating in those groups. If you're engaging in several different groups, you'll definitely want a way to track your results more formally so that you can compare your participation and outcomes on paper.

When I organize my spreadsheet for tracking my participation in groups, I typically record:

- Name of the event or group
- Group or event contacts (another great place to organize and cross-reference contacts)
- Group or event fees/dues
- Payment period (single event, annual, month to month, etc.)
- Membership period (single event, annual, month to month, etc.)

- Additional expenses (meals, display materials for events, parking, etc.)
- Time spent (meetings, travel, special events, etc.)
- Referrals generated
- Income generated
- Notes

Again, some of these categories are self-explanatory, but a few merit clarification.

Because we're getting into the nitty-gritty of tracking expenses and outcomes, when you're documenting the groups you're participating in, you'll want to detail the financial investment of your involvement. This includes not only registration fees (for events) and membership dues, but the payment schedule and any additional expenses related to taking part in the group. Some groups have a membership fee and expect members to pay an additional fee for room rental as part of their participation. Other groups hold meetings over the lunch hour or even after hours, when members partake in a meal or drinks as part of the social engagement. Some groups meet at locations that don't have free parking, or perhaps you're Ubering to and from meetings. All those expenses should be accounted for when tracking your investment in an organization or event.

I also like to break down the payment schedule for any groups I'm joining. While I typically amortize my business expenses over 12 months to suit my monthly budgeting, it's nice to know when large, single payments are going to crop up. Even though the expense is the same for a single membership payment versus a month-to-month billing, if the membership fee is high enough, and the returns are low enough, I might decide that a group isn't a good fit for me based on the inflexibility of payment structure alone.

Basically, if I'm on the fence about joining an organization—whether it's fun and engaging, or supporting my goals and objectives—then a detail as small as being able to pay what I want, when I want is enough to push me one way or the other.

I belong to a women's professional networking group here in the Denver area. The group is great, the caliber of members is top-notch, and I've made some fabulous connections. The annual membership isn't onerous (less than $200). But, I have to travel nearly an hour each way, so there's a gas expense. And, there's a luncheon fee of $25 each month in addition to the annual membership. Added to that is the "after-lunch casual networking" in the bar area with the expense of a drink (alcoholic or nonalcoholic). So, while the annual membership and the additional monthly fees are affordable, they do start to add up.

When you're deciding if a group is a good fit for you and your business, consider whether:

- It's a place you're excited go to and happy to make time for
- Other members are going to support your goals and contribute to your success
- The logistics of the group meet your needs

These "soft features" of an organization are just as important, if not more so, than the leads and referrals that might come out of your participation. Because if you don't want to be there, or you start to skip meetings because they're boring and a waste of time, then you've wasted your financial investment.

Referrals and income generated from your participation in a group are a more precise measure of success than your feelings (after all, you can love a group and its members and never get a single lead from it). You can organize this data in whatever way suits you and your business. Do you want to track leads by month? Do you want to keep a running total? However you arrange the information, you'll be much more successful if you put dollars to the data as frequently as possible. This is easily done when you can tie a client or project back to a specific referral from a specific introduction in a specific group or event. You can track referrals by simply recording the number of leads you've received from members of a group, and then transitioning them to projects or clients when the time comes.

At LunchingwithLions.com, download a simple spreadsheet set up for tracking your participation in events or groups. But, as with everything else I've shared with you, there's no right or wrong way to document your participation, investment, and outcomes. I encourage you to design a system that works best for you.

Last, make note of the amount of time your participation in the group requires. Record the time for each meeting, as well as travel time and any prep or debrief time you need. The professional women's organization I mentioned previously is great fun and very much fits my goals and objectives. On paper, the meetings are once a month and last two hours. But (big "but") the travel time is nearly an hour each way and, after the formal two-hour luncheon meeting, members frequently stay at the venue and move to the bar area for casual networking. Even though the organization is great and I love participating in it, I'm watching my results closely—because a two-hour meeting is really more like six hours when I figure in all the travel and schmoozing time.

REFERRALS AND INCOME

When you create your tracking system, consider adding a separate spreadsheet or process flow for tracking referrals and income alone. This, after all, is the nut of why you're networking. Understanding the results you're generating in terms of new clients and projects over the long term is what will keep you motivated and demonstrate why you're investing your time and money in networking in the first place.

I once had coffee with a unicorn. Well, he wasn't an actual unicorn, but he was pretty unique. The conversation turned to networking, as it often does with me, and I asked him where he was networking.

> **Me:** So, what groups are you part of and where do you find your referrals?
>
> **Unicorn:** I get 26 percent of my business from Group A and 32 percent of my business from Group B. I've recently joined Group C and I'm seeing an increase of two to four referrals that are converting to sales each month, so I'm going to stick with that one for a while too. The rest of my business comes from Group D.

Oh, myyyyyyy. He was speaking my love language, people! This was a man who was clearly tracking the outcomes of the time and energy he spends networking and tweaking his activities to maximize his efforts.

What would it mean to you to have that kind of clarity about your results?

When I track my referrals and income, I include the following information:

- Date
- Contact name (who brought me the lead)

- Contact reference (how I know that person, through what group or event)
- Lead name
- Lead email
- Lead phone
- Lead business name
- Lead website
- Estimated value of the lead (this is easier when the lead ties directly to a project or client)
- Percentage of overall income (how much of your business this new client or project represents)
- Date of first contact (with lead)
- Date of next contact (with lead)
- Notes and follow-up

When tracking leads, you'll definitely want to know who passed you the referral so that you can follow up to thank them or give them updates about how the new relationship is progressing. I like to record where that connection came from because it helps me better understand what types of engagement are paying off in my networking—groups, events, introductions, etc.

Note all the relevant information for a lead when you receive it from your contact. You'll want multiple ways to establish contact, and you'll want a way to "stalk" your lead before connecting so that you can get familiar with them.

If your business is B2C, scope out your lead's social media and see what interests them. Take a look at their profile picture so that you recognize them immediately if you opt to meet in person. Learn a little bit about them so that you can ask relevant questions and lay the path to be known, liked, and trusted just a little bit faster.

If your business is B2B, do your due diligence by learning about your lead's business. Research their industry and get an idea on best practices with regards to their service or product so that you can offer constructive suggestions to your lead immediately. Get familiar with your lead's LinkedIn network and social media so that you can comment on content they've shared and build that trust factor.

Once a lead transitions from a referral to an honest-to-God contract, project, or sale, first record the value of the lead and assign it a percentage of your overall income. There are a couple reasons for this. First and foremost, you'll have tangible, recorded evidence of the results of your networking efforts. When you know what you're achieving, you can measure your outcomes against your goals, your budgets, and your investments, and you can gauge the success of your hard work.

Second, you may start to see patterns in your leads that you can leverage for even greater income. Maybe you have a certain contact who is funneling you a significant number of new projects or clients. Recognizing them with special follow-up gifts or recognition can help maintain that positive relationship. Likewise, if you see that your new business is falling into certain service areas, you can revisit your messaging to make sure you're adequately communicating all that you do.

As with your contact database, tracking the dates of when you connect with your lead and being purposeful and intentional about following up with them through your sales process will ensure a more successful engagement and transition from referral to project or client. Maintaining accurate and up-to-date notes will help you make sure that you stay on top of the sales conversation and that you don't drop the ball on any promised information or deliverable. We'll talk more about follow-ups in the next chapter.

By now, you should be seeing how these tracking systems are interrelated. Tracking your results from multiple angles shows you how your networking efforts are building on themselves. A sustained effort in groups results in introductions and contacts, which grow into relationships. Relationships are tied to leads and referrals. Your leads and referrals become clients. Clients mean income.

Following the trail backward from income shows the relationships and organizations that are generating the greatest results and lets you focus your resources (Time! Money!) in the places that get you the highest return.

Prompts and Activities

- Download my networking tracking spreadsheets from LunchingwithLions.com.

- Customize your trackers with the information you need for your goals.

HELLO
my name is

Chapter 17

FOLLOW UP AND EVALUATE

Networking is about relationships, and relationships are social contracts that are based on mutual benefits. Give and take. You give, they take. They give, you take.

"Take" seems like kind of a greedy word, doesn't it? How about we replace it with one of its synonyms, like "receive" or "succeed."

You give, they *receive*.

They give, you *succeed*.

Mmmmmmm, those are much yummier! Because, really, that's what we're talking about here. When you and your network support each other by passing leads and referrals, you're enabling each other's success.

Which is why, in order to build effective networking relationships, you need to carry it beyond the initial meeting, beyond the one-on-one connection, and beyond the exchange of leads or business. You need to create a system of follow-ups that nurture your relationships and provide fertile ground for your proverbial orchard to grow.

I'm going to talk in detail about nurturing your networking in Chapter 19. But for now, I want to talk about creating a system for following up with your network once you've established a relationship, and you're working together as collaborators, referral partners, power partners, etc.

FOLLOW-UPS

So far, when we've talked about tracking your results, I've specifically suggested keeping track of your last interaction with a contact, the length of time since your last interaction, your next scheduled interaction, and notes about your interactions. The reason I do this is because it is so, so easy to lose time in our businesses. Believe me! I jot down a "to-do" and before I know it, six weeks have gone by, and it's still a "not-done"!

Which is why I'm a big proponent of systems. They keep us on track, and they make the doing easier. Ding! A reminder pops up to do the thing. We do the thing. It's done and we're still on track. No brain cells were lost in the doing of this thing.

I. Love. Systems.

When we think about creating a system for following up with our network, I like to consider:

- How important/relevant is this person to my goals and objectives? (Connectors, Collaborators, and Clients)
- Do I have specific ways in which this person can serve me immediately? (Connectors and Contractors)
- Do I have specific ways in which I can serve this person immediately? (Collaborators and Clients)
- Is this person a valuable connection to have in the community? (Connectors and Master Connectors)

- Does this person have things to teach me? (Collaborators and Contractors)
- How much do I enjoy this person's company? (all, especially Cool Kids)

Then, I map out a follow-up system for each type of connection. Developing a system is as easy as asking yourself a series of questions. I usually start like this:

If I meet someone at an event or group and they're important or relevant to my goals and objectives:

Are they a connector, collaborator, or client?
If they're a client, how will I engage with them beyond the first meeting? A coffee? A lunch? A video call?
If, after the second one-on-one meeting, they're interested but not ready to buy, how soon will I follow up with them?
What form will that follow-up take? An email? A call?
If they respond to the follow-up, what's my plan?
If they don't respond to the follow up, how long will I wait to reach out to them again?
What form will that take?

Or, it might look like this:

If I meet someone at an event or group and they're important or relevant to my goals and objectives as a collaborator:
How will I engage with them beyond the first meeting? A coffee? A lunch? A video call?
Is there a specific reason to set a second one-on-one connection immediately (for example, a collaborative project or busi-

ness arrangement)? If not, what's my timeframe for connecting a second time?

What form will that connection take?

How frequently will I attempt to connect with this person?

What form will those connections take?

Once you have an idea of the frequency of follow-ups with the different types of connections you're making, note them in your contact database and create some sort of prompt to get those steps done. A simple Google Calendar reminder each week can be a simple and effective way to start.

As you can tell, it's not an exact science. In fact, you may wind up tweaking your follow-up schedule based on individual conversations or occurrences when you do connect with your network. Some connections, on paper, may look identical, but for personal reasons, you connect with one more frequently and more deeply than another.

EVALUATING YOUR RESULTS

Back in Chapter 3, I asked you to set some SMART goals (Specific, Measurable, Actionable, Realistic, and Timebound). Guess what. By tracking your results, you can measure (*M!*) your success.

Here's where you may want to tweak the data you're tracking. I can nag you all day about tracking your investment and the value of your leads, but if that data isn't tied to what you want to achieve, it's worthless to you. (Of course, I'm just assuming that, as a business owner, your goals somehow center around income and lead generation, but who am I to know?)

Because you set specific, measurable goals, you'll be able to track your outcomes. Maybe your goal was to increase your network by 50 percent. Great! Track your contacts, count the number of new names on your list, and do the math. Or perhaps your goal was to increase lead generation by 100 percent in your business. Fab! Track the leads you're gaining from networking and referrals, and (again!) do the math.

Whatever your goals are, when you set SMART ones and create the right tools to track results, you're able to evaluate your success against your investment of time and money.

HOW OFTEN SHOULD YOU TRACK RESULTS?

Because networking is (say it with me!) a long game, you'll want to measure results on a quarterly, six-month, or yearly basis. Any shorter time periods might not accurately reflect the overall picture. On the flip side, you'll want to track your networking activities every day that you engage in them.

Going to a group or event? Come home and track your activities as part of your after-event process (which also includes things like connecting with new contacts on LinkedIn, sending thank-you notes, and sharing the event on social media). Having a one-on-one with a new connection? Come home, make notes, and set a follow-up date in your planner.

The most important thing to remember in this process is to be aware: Aware of your goals and objectives for networking. And aware of what types of connections you're making so that you can be purposeful and intentional in your activities. Creating the systems and processes for tracking your results keeps you aware of your progress. It reminds you when to follow up to maintain fertile contacts so that you can measure success—and count the apples in that flourishing orchard.

Prompts and Activities

- Download my networking tracking spreadsheets from LunchingwithLions.com and customize them for your goals.

- Download my communications map worksheet from LunchingwithLions.com to help you create your follow-up and nurture messaging.

HELLO
my name is

Chapter 18

HOW LONG MUST I NETWORK?

O ne of the questions I get asked most often is "How long is this networking thing going to take?"

After I stop laughing, I usually answer, "Until."

You keep networking *until*.

- *Until* you're getting a steady stream of leads from your connections
- *Until* you're getting leads from your connections' connections
- *Until* you're getting referrals from so many sources you're no longer sure which are the result of networking
- *Until* you've reached your goals and objectives

Shockingly, this answer doesn't always go over too well. See, we humans are into immediate gratification. We want to see a direct result of our efforts, and we want to see them now. It's what keeps us excited and motivated. This is especially true for entrepreneurs and business owners who suffer from the "shiny penny" syndrome. We're easily distracted when the task at hand isn't engaging us fully.

Listen, I get it. I know intellectually that networking takes time. A lot of time. And even I get frustrated by that. It would be great to attend an event or group meeting, introduce myself, have a few conversations, sign a few deals, and be done. Check that group off my list and move on to the next.

I wish it were that easy.

I don't think it's a coincidence that the people who ask me how long networking will take are usually the same people who tell me about their bootyless state despite their seemingly never-ending networking efforts. When I start to ask questions, I generally find that the problem isn't one of reality (they really *are* networking their booty off) but rather of perception (they just *think* they're networking their booty off).

So, what's going on?

The reality is that networking is a numbers game, plain and simple. You have to engage with a certain number of people before you reach the tipping point and start to generate the referrals and leads that will support your success.

When people ask me "How long?" or lament the loss of their booty, what they're really asking is, "How many people do I have to talk to before I see results?" That, my friend, is a question I can answer!

We've talked about organizing your contacts and tracking referrals and income. But if you want to get super granular on your networking efforts, I encourage you to track actual conversations and engagements.

Why? Tracking your engagements and conversations—and when they turn into leads—gives you the data you need to calculate your conversion rate. Your conversion rate then gives you a clear goal to work toward. Let me show you.

YOUR CONVERSION RATE

Let's say you start to document your conversations and engagements. At the end of the first month, you've had 24 conversations that have directly led to two referrals.

When we divide your leads/referrals by the number of conversations it took to generate them, it looks like this:

$$\frac{2 \text{ LEADS/REFERRALS}}{24 \text{ CONVERSATIONS}} = 8\% \text{ CONVERSION}$$

That means that 8 percent of your conversations should generate a lead. So, if you want 10 leads a month, you'll need to engage in at least 120 conversations a month. If you want five leads a week, you'll have to have at least 60 conversations a week.

This same formula can be used to determine your closing rate on leads. Taking the 10 leads a month from above, we'll estimate that you close (contract signed, deposit paid) one lead in the same month:

$$\frac{1 \text{ SALE}}{10 \text{ LEADS}} = 10\% \text{ CLOSE RATE}$$

Now you can estimate how many conversations you need to be having in order to reach your sales goal. For instance, if you want 10 sales in a month, you should be having 1,200 conversations.

Right about now is when my clients start to hyperventilate a little bit. Because those numbers are daunting. I mean, there are only 720 hours in a month (fewer in February!). How on earth can you expect to have 1,200 conversations in that time?

Deep breaths, friend. Let me soothe some of your worries.

The effects of networking are cumulative if you stick with it.

The effects of networking are cumulative if you stick with it. In other words, when you first join a group or an organization, your schedule will fill up with one-on-one conversations as you get to know the other group members more intimately. But, because you're focusing on the Five Cs and the most strategic connections for your goals, you can be efficient in your individual get-togethers and soon your time commitment will be reduced to meeting times and a few one-on-one check-ins during the month. Once you've built individual relationships with your targets within the group, showing up and engaging in the meetings themselves will substitute for more personal conversations. Then, you can focus on nurturing the relationships that best support your goals.

Keep in mind also that "conversations" take different forms. The purpose of a conversation is to stay top of mind with your contact, so a simple phone call, engagement on social media, or personal email may be enough to generate one of those leads. In Chapter 19, I talk in detail about how you can nurture your connections to achieve that top-of-mind status and keep your network healthy and productive.

Solopreneurs and small-business owners often think they want all the business, but in reality, they can handle only a certain number of contracts or clients at any one time, depending on their product or service. This is an area in which awareness is key. Being aware of your goals and objectives in your business, and your capacity to serve your clients well, should form the basis of your sales goals. So, while 10 sales per month sounds like a giant failure if you're a retail giant, 10 sales per month may be more than you can realistically handle if you're a solopreneur.

One more note on awareness as we discuss sales. Your goals and objectives for networking may not have anything to do with sales. You may be trying to grow your network overall, or create brand recognition in your market, or have some other goal completely unrelated to leads and sales. In that case, you may be able to use the same formula and replace the variables with the data that you're desiring to track in order to calculate your own results.

I believe wholeheartedly that networking and referrals are the number-one best marketing tools for small-business owners and entrepreneurs. Earlier, I said that networking *amplifies* your brand, because the people you meet and with whom you build relationships become spokespersons for you and what you have to offer (as you do for them). The beauty of networking is that the time you spend building those relationships lasts infinitely longer than a single marketing campaign or promotion. People don't have a time limit on how long they like you.

Nurturing your network and sustaining those relationships also sustains that amplification of your brand. I have people I recommend today whom I met years ago. They're still getting business out of our relationship. *That's* what I call a good ROI.

The quality of the leads you generate through personal relationships is far and above those you gain through social media, email marketing, or digital advertising. While those channels have far greater reach and can spread your message to many more people, they're no match for the value of a genuine, personal referral.

Networking can and will lead to success if you commit to it for the long term, create a plan based on your objectives and goals, and track your results so that you can align your activities with the best outcomes.

Prompts and Activities

Look back through your calendar for the last 90 to 120 days.

- How many networking events or groups have you been to?

- How many one-on-ones have you had?

- Can you track any leads or referrals to those engagements?

- Use the data at hand to calculate your conversion rate today (as you increase your networking, this number will get clearer—but you have to start somewhere).

HELLO
my name is
Chapter 19

NURTURING YOUR NETWORK

Now that you're really working that networking circuit, how do you manage all those new connections you've built? How do you nurture your network? How do you tend the soil that allows your orchard of relationships to thrive?

In my observation, it's in the nurturing of networks that a lot of business owners fall down on the job. There tends to be a "wham-bam-thank-you-ma'am" approach to networking. I meet you at an event, we connect, we schedule a one-on-one, we hit it off, and then...crickets. Maybe we run into each other at a future event or meeting, and it's kind of awkward. Or, maybe we don't, and all those potential connections are just...lost.

It's kind of like a "one-lunch" stand. (Ha! See what I did there?) Anyhoo...

If you want to grow a healthy orchard, you have to till the soil, fertilize it, water it, and weed it. You have to support your little saplings until they grow strong enough to stand on their own. You have to graft healthy materials to those trees that are struggling. You have to cultivate the orchard to get the fruits that you want.

Long story short, it's not enough to meet, connect, and learn about each other. Those exchanges do not a relationship make. The types of mutually beneficial relationships that networking is based on require long-term attention.

When I say that, do you cringe a little? Are you thinking how much work it'll be to integrate all these new contacts into your world? Wondering how on earth you'll manage all the lunches and coffees? Stressing over the time it'll take?

When we're aware of our goals, we can discard activities that don't serve our purposes.

Throughout this book, I've been encouraging (begging) you to create awareness, purpose, and intent around your networking activities. When we're aware of our goals and objectives in our business, we can be purposeful and intentional about aligning our activities to reach those goals. Part of this alignment is discarding activities that don't serve our purposes.

Networking is the same. When we're purposeful and intentional about the connections we're making, we make better connections. Fewer connections. Quality over quantity, remember? And these fewer, higher-quality connections will be with people:

- Who support our success
- With whom we can build long-term, mutually beneficial relationships
- With whom we can build rapport over time

Here's the thing. When we genuinely care about people, it doesn't feel like work to keep in touch with them. That's why it seems so effortless to ring up our friends from high school regularly or keep those quarterly lunch dates with former coworkers and managers. When we appreciate people for what they've brought into our lives, either personally or professionally, we naturally nurture those relationships in an authentic way. When we do that, we're tending to our orchard. And a healthy orchard yields tasty fruit.

Okay. I'm kinda tired of the orchard analogy now.

What we're talking about here is fostering long-term relationships with the connections you've been building. If you don't need that connection right this minute, how do you lay the groundwork so that, a year or two from now, you can call on them for a professional favor?

Let's talk about some strategies for laying those foundations.

PRIORITIZE YOUR CONNECTIONS

I touched on this when talking about systematizing your contacts. When we're aware of who we're connecting with, we can categorize our connections into the Five Cs (Connector, Collaborator, Contractor, Client, Cool Kids). Doing this allows us to figure out the best way to allocate our attention.

Likewise, identifying who are funneling significant numbers of leads and referrals our way allows us to prioritize specific beneficial relationships and bump certain people to the head of the "love 'em up" line.

SHOW YOU CARE

We're one fifth of the way through the twenty-first century, and the interwebs makes it sooooo easy to stay in touch with our connections and informed about what's going on in their lives and businesses. The key here is to stay in the orbit of your network so that you remain top of mind if you require their assistance—or they require yours—down the road. Use emails, social media, phone calls, coffee dates, and social gatherings to maintain that connection. Resource suggestion: One of my very favorite tools (without which I'd probably never get around to thank-yous) is SendOut-Cards.com. This service makes it super easy to write and send cards, and it allows you to upload designs for your brand.

DON'T RELY ON SOCIAL MEDIA

Sure, everyone's doing it. But...everyone's doing it. Just as talking on the phone isn't as intimate as an in-person chat, social media doesn't have the same power as more personal modes of connection. Sharing, commenting, and liking posts is great. Reaching out with a phone call or a handwritten note when you see that a friend or past colleague has changed jobs or received a promotion is better.

BE (AUTHENTICALLY) HELPFUL

From sharing articles that your contacts might find valuable to offering to connect a friend's son with a potential internship, look for ways to be helpful to your network. Be authentic, don't over-promise, and don't offer to help with the ulterior motive of calling in a favor at a later date.

DON'T FORCE IT

I hope you're sitting down for this. Sweet Pea, not everyone is going to like you all the time. If you've been trying to connect with someone, and you're getting crickets in return, be like Elsa from *Frozen* and let it go. Maybe they've changed direction, or maybe they're swamped, or maybe their spam filter is just super touchy. Or, maybe they just don't want to maintain a relationship with you. Don't be needy. Just. Let. It. Go.

REEVALUATE OCCASIONALLY

As you reach your SMART goals, or as your business evolves, the types of relationships you'll need to support your success may change. When you're strategizing for your business, build in time to evaluate your networking goals, the people you're connecting with, and the way you're doing it. Remember, when we're aware of what we want, we can be purposeful and intentional in going after it.

To summarize, and to help you start building your nurturing process, here's what I suggest:

- Prioritize your contacts.
- Reach out to each of your contacts personally (outside of social media) a minimum of four times a year to stay connected (more frequently for higher-priority connections).
- Schedule these connections and add reminders to your calendar.
- Send birthday, anniversary, and holiday greetings via email or snail mail.
- Connect on social media regularly.
- Invite contacts to have coffee, lunch, or happy-hour drinks, or to attend an event with you.

Like most people, setting aside time for one-on-one connections is a real challenge. If you, too, are time challenged (ha!), I'll share a little trick that I use.

About once a month, I'll reach out to a bunch of mid-level contacts (i.e., not top-priority ones, but people with whom I like to maintain somewhat regular connection) and invite them to come have coffee with me. Then, I find a local coffee shop and settle in for a few hours. I sit with my computer, and my connections come in and out at their scheduled times. If I'm feeling generous, I'll even tell the barista to charge all the drinks to me, and I'll pay at the end of the afternoon.

This saves me tons of travel time (Time! Money!), and enables me to knock out a bunch of "connects" all at once. If I'm unable to fill all my slots ahead of time, I'll post to my business page that I'm having "open office hours," and I'll have people sign up for half-hour or hour-long slots at no charge. It's a win-win. I save time, and I make myself available to a lot of people efficiently. I encourage you to think about using this tactic in your networking.

Nurturing your network is an often-overlooked but vital part of your networking plan. Avoid those awkward encounters after a one-lunch stand, and build the relationships that will support your success by creating a follow-up and nurturing system that works for both you and your network.

Plant the seed. Eat the apples.

(Okay. No more orchard. I promise.)

Prompts and Activities

Create a list and a plan for nurturing the most valuable connections in your network based on your goals.

- How often will you reach out?

- What form will those contacts take? A card? A phone call? A giftie?

- Is this something you can outsource, or will you manage it yourself?

- How will you organize your nurturing plan? Top 10? Top 25? Who gets what and when?

THE ONE WITH ALL THE TIPS

"Touchy-feely." "Hokey." "Hippie-dippie." These are words and phrases I use regularly to explain to people what I'm *not*. I'm a fairly left-brained, pragmatic gal. I like systems and procedures and step-by-step instructions. Checklists make my heart sing. Order is my happy place.

But (big "but" here), as I've said, networking was an emotional minefield for me. It brought up all the mindjunk and insecurities of my life as a Professional New Girl. Just the idea of getting out there made me shake in my Uggs.

Which is why, when I started my personal networking challenge, I had a really hard time. Because I wanted an instruction manual. *How* do I network? *How* do I find the groups? *How* do I make myself get out of the car when what I really want to do is turn around and go home? *How* do I walk into a big room full of scary, not-friendly strangers? What's the system? What's the next step I need to follow? Gimme a process.

I wanted someone to give me the steps to follow so that I didn't have to think about the pain of the process—so that I could instead focus on building that networking muscle. Like hiring a personal trainer when you really want to learn how to use the weight machines and build a solid gym habit that you love. You want to get results. I was looking for a networking coach to show me the ropes, and I wasn't finding anything.

So, I went out, walked through the emotional fire, got good at it, and then I wrote a book about it. *This* book (hi!). And the purpose of this book is to give you specific steps, strategies, and systems you can follow. Because I found that once I had sussed out *how* to network, it got a lot easier emotionally.

And so, I introduce to you, dear reader, the chapter with all the tips! Ta-da!

As with everything else in this book, these are suggestions that you can take or leave, depending on your business goals and objectives, and what feels right to you. I guarantee you'll find some of them helpful in tackling the practical and emotional challenges of networking, so I encourage you to give them a try.

I've broken these tips into different categories:
- For before, during, and after an event or meeting
- For follow-ups and one-on-ones
- For nurturing your network

And, now, without further ado: TIPS FOR SUCCESSFUL NETWORKING!

BEFORE THE EVENT OR MEETING

1. **Find the right group.** Do your research to find the group that aligns with your business objectives. Ask your clients where they're networking. Visit the websites and Facebook pages of the organizations and events you find interesting.

Dig a little deeper into the group's purpose to find out if it's a good fit for your goals.

2. **Research the event.** Read the comments posted after the last event, look at pictures, and read the event descriptions. There are lots of clues available online that will give you a feel for what to expect. Reach out to the hostess or another member of the group you may know in order to ask about the event and what to expect.

3. **Identify your targets.** Peruse the RSVP lists and membership lists of the events and organizations you're interested in visiting. What types of businesses are on the lists? Remember, you want to avoid networking with other people in your industry. So, if you're a life coach and there are six other life coaches signed up for an event, that might be one you want to skip this month. However, if a group is chock full of members who fit your ideal client profile, sign up now!

4. **RSVP.** Most event listings these days allow you to RSVP (yes, no, or interested/maybe). If you know you're going to attend, please RSVP. As a group organizer myself, I love when people commit early because it allows me to organize the best possible event . I can set up the room, make sure I have enough materials, and prepare learning activities suitable for the group size. Likewise, if something comes up and you're unable to attend, change your RSVP. Bonus points if you send the hostess your regrets and explain why you can't make it.

5. **Introduce yourself.** Take advantage of online groups and introduce yourself and your business before an event. In

the same way that you're making a list of people with whom you hope to connect, this gives other people a heads-up that you'll be in attendance, in case they want to connect with you. Plus, by engaging with other members online before you meet face-to-face, you can minimize some of that social anxiety. You'll feel as if you already know them!

6. **Check your upcoming calendar.** Before you attend an event, look ahead a few weeks on your calendar. How much time do you have available for follow-up meetings? Can you swing face-to-face coffees, or would it be better to schedule 30-minute video calls? Do you need to prioritize the top two meetings you hope to secure, or can your schedule handle more in-person get-togethers? Understanding your availability *before* you start connecting will help you focus your efforts. And, don't be afraid to say, "I'm booked up the next few weeks. Could we look at [Insert Date Two to Three Weeks Out]?"

7. **Set a goal for follow-ups.** Once you've checked your calendar for availability, you can set a goal for the number of follow-ups you want to come away with, and you can prioritize who you schedule additional time with. If you're attending multiple events each week (6.3 hours, people), you'll want to have a clear idea of how many follow-ups you want to generate from each so that you don't overwhelm your calendar and yourself.

8. **Get your networking kit together.** There are a few things I make sure to have with me for any networking engagement.

    a. **Business cards:** Business cards today are cheap and easy to order online, so in my opinion, there's no excuse for ever being without one. If you've just set up your business or you don't have a logo and visual brand yet, you can order simple, clean cards that have your name, email, and phone number on them. Put simply, you *must* have a business card to leave with your contacts. This is nonnegotiable.

b. **Name tag:** Most events provide stick-on name tags, which work just fine. I invested in a permanent magnetic name tag (with rhinestones) that includes my logo, my name, and my business titles (Business Coach, Founder of WEBO Network). Having a permanent, branded name tag falls under the looking-like-you-have-your-sh*t-together category. It's one more piece of visible evidence that you take yourself and your business seriously—and they should too.

c. **Flyers/Handouts for featured programs:** When I'm promoting a program or event of my own, I make sure to have a stack of handouts available to share with my connections. Providing them with all the pertinent details and information—in the same way that a business card does—is much more likely to result in further engagement than telling them to check your website for details.

d. **Notebook:** I actually never go anywhere in life without a little notebook because I can't remember anything. And I *always* take one when I'm networking. I jot down notes when people give their introductions so that I know why I want to connect with them. If somebody forgot their business card, I can offer to write down their name and number so that I can follow up with them later. Also, when I'm at a networking event, my mind usually starts to race because I'm meeting all of these amazing people who are doing all of these amazing things. It's like super juice. It gets me thinking and scheming about my business. It's always good to have a small notebook with you to write down your inspirations.

9. **Dress the part.** Personal branding with your wardrobe has become a hot topic in the last few years. Aligning your look with the promise you're making to your clients is really important. Have you ever noticed that bankers and mortgage brokers are typically the most professionally dressed attendees at any networking event? Hello! They work with your money. They know that people feel more comfortable handing their money to someone who is professional and polished, so they dress the part. Think about your brand and your ideal clients. How can you best present yourself to connect with them and reinforce the promise of what they can expect when working with you?

10. **Grounding/Affirmations.** Feeling nervous before an event? Practice your affirmations and controlled breathing. Ask yourself: What do I want to project in the next hour? How do I want to feel? Select three words and repeat them to yourself as you deep breathe on the 4-4-8 counts. Give yourself a pep talk. Whatever works for you, take the time to do a little self-care to soothe your anxieties before an event or meeting so that you present your best, most confident self.

AT THE EVENT

1. **Don't arrive too early.** It's awkward, and conversation is always disrupted as new people arrive. Time your arrival to whenever you think 50–75 percent of the people are already going to be there. That makes it easy to kind of slip in a little bit and find your place. (Hint: This is a good question to ask the hostess during a pre-event connection.)

2. **Introduce yourself to the hostess.** It's always good to know the person in charge. She's gone to a lot of trouble to plan and facilitate this event, so let her know how excited you are to be there. If you emailed her with questions prior to the event, this is a great time to thank her for her response. Don't be shy about telling her if you're feeling nervous or uncertain. She knows everyone there. A good hostess will make sure to introduce you to a few people and help you feel more comfortable.

3. **Volunteer to help with a task.** This is a great strategy, especially if you're feeling nervous or out of place. Ask the hostess if you can help by passing out name tags (you're going to meet people really fast if you're the one doing this).

4. **Wear something distinctive, such as a bright color or a fabulous piece of jewelry.** It gives people something to comment on when they approach you, makes you stand out from the crowd, and helps people remember you. If you follow up and they don't remember who you are, you can always prompt them by saying "I was the one with the necklace."

5. **Offer a compliment to people you meet, and be sincere about it.** Everyone loves flattery, so use it whenever you can. It might be something someone's wearing, or something you've heard about them, or their business, or even the design of their business card. Call attention to something that you think is fabulous, and they'll really appreciate it.

6. **Label people.** This is helpful, as long as you don't do it in a negative, snarky way! As people introduce themselves, catalog them by whether they're Connectors, Collaborators, Contractors, Clients, or Cool Kids. Prioritize those people you want to engage with further, and maneuver yourself so that you can achieve that. If you've targeted them ahead of the event, approach them during the open networking time, introduce yourself, and let them know you've been looking forward to meeting them.

7. **Hang out near the food.** This is my favorite! Everyone's going to be there.

8. **Take a seat with other people.** Don't go off and sit by yourself at the end of the table where nobody else is sitting because you think that people will come and sit next to you. Nope. Put yourself between two people or across from people who are already there, and then immediately introduce yourself to them. Don't wait for people to approach you. When you create the introductions, you control and create a group. Whether they knew each other before, you all know each other now, and your group's going to rock.

9. **Focus on the person immediately to each side and in front of you.** There's nothing worse than feeling as though

the person you're speaking with would rather be somewhere else. So, give your conversation partners your full attention.

10. **Ask questions.** Once somebody starts speaking, odds are you're going to find an opportunity to ask a question or two, which will give you a chance to reveal your personality and share common interests. If you're nervous, introduce yourself to someone, ask them a question about either them or their business, and then listen. Enjoy their story, think about what they're saying, and don't worry about you. Eventually there will be a natural opening for you to comment on yourself or your business.

11. **Be an active listener.** People love to talk about their business, what they do, and all their amazing interests. Actually, talking about those things is pretty much the reason why they're at that event. And, really, who doesn't like to be listened to? Who doesn't like an audience to appreciate them and think that they're pretty cool? While you're listening, watch out for your resting bitch face (because we can get so caught up in the story that our RBF comes on strong). Remember to smile, nod, and be an active listener.

12. **Be respectful of the introduction time limit.** We've all been to events where people droned on, and on, and on about themselves and their business. Remember, be engaging and direct with your elevator speech—who you are, what you do, whom you serve, and what makes you different. Practice, practice, practice before you arrive so that you can tailor your delivery to the time limit (if you connected with the hostess before the event, ask her how

much time you should plan for). And, keep your call to action to a single ask. Don't overload your audience with a whole to-do list.

13. **Be enthusiastic about what you do.** Don't downplay your personal acumen or business offering. If you're not excited and passionate about it, who will be? Remember, you are your brand's ambassador, and it's up to you to spread its awesomeness in the world.

14. **Check in with yourself.** If this is your first time visiting an organization or event, check in with yourself to see how you're feeling. Are you engaged in the conversation around you? Is it the type of conversation you were hoping for/expecting? What types of people are at the event, and how are they interacting? Are you having fun? Are you excited about coming back? There are a million networking opportunities in the world today, so you don't have to stay in a group that isn't enjoyable or that isn't going to further your objectives.

15. **Always thank the hostess of the event on the way out.** Ask her how you can join the mailing list, if you haven't already done so. Ask her about the next event, and make plans to connect with her on social media. Ask her for a follow-up coffee if she's someone who aligns with your objectives. She knows everyone at the event, so she's a good ally in your networking efforts. She can connect you to people both during and after the event, as well as before the next event.

16. **Follow up right away.** The best networkers are the ones who work it. Take notes, follow up, take the relationship

to the next level with coffee or lunch, build relationships— get the business. Have your calendar out and ready at the event and make the strategic connections that will help you further your goals. Take the list of Connectors, Collaborators, Contractors, Clients, and Cool Kids you created during the elevator speeches, and get to work setting up one-on-one coffees and calls. Don't leave until you have the most important follow-up engagements set on your calendar and theirs. It's that simple.

AFTER THE EVENT

1. **Thank the hostess or organization again.** If you didn't join the group's Facebook, Meetup, or LinkedIn page before the event, do so now. Write a post thanking them for a great event, and be specific about what you got out of it ("The demonstration of the newest double-wheeled unicycles was a real treat!"). Groups and organizations use this type of feedback to improve their events for members.

2. **Connect with new contacts on social media.** Stay in touch with the people you met at the event. When you get back to your office, check out their websites, sign up for their email lists, like/follow them on social media (Facebook, Twitter, Instagram, etc.), and check out their LinkedIn profiles. Reach out through LinkedIn for a connection, reminding them of your recent meeting; for example, "Hi, [Insert Name]. It was lovely to meet you at today's Unicyclists United meeting. Your comments about advances in single-chain dynamics really got me thinking. I'd like to add you to my professional network."

3. **Add contacts to your customer relationship manager (CRM).** Go through the cards you collected and add names and details to your CRM or spreadsheet. Remember, you can't add people to your mailing list unless you've specifically asked their permission. Catalog your new contacts under Connectors, Collaborators, Contractors, Clients, and Cool Kids. Once you've reviewed their websites and social media, decide if you need to follow up with anyone, and make the calls. Track activities in your CRM so that you have a record of your interactions and the results.

FOLLOW-UPS AND ONE-ON-ONES

1. **Be clear about your expectations.** If you're the one setting the date, be specific about what you're looking for. Are you looking for referrals? Do you want an entrepreneur's advice on starting your own business? Whatever your reason for wanting to connect, let your contact know what you're hoping for.

2. **It doesn't have to be coffee.** I once met a contact for ice cream and short walk around the block. The point is that you're setting aside dedicated, uninterrupted time to make your connection. One caveat: Avoid alcohol until you get to know someone better. While a drink can lubricate the social stress of networking, it can also lower your inhibitions enough that you don't present your best self.

3. **Do your homework.** There are plenty of ways these days to learn about your new contact before you meet face-to-face. Do a little research by visiting their LinkedIn profile, Twitter feed, Facebook page(s), and any other social media channels to get an idea about their business and their brand.

Read their website, especially the "About" page to learn more about them and their story. Flatter your contact by showing genuine interest in something you've read about them. Because, as we all know, flattery will get you everywhere!

4. **Take a business card.** Do I have to remind you? Yes, because I've been to plenty of events and one-on-ones where someone showed up without a business card. Even if you're 110 percent sure that the person already has your card in their possession, be prepared to hand them a new one. And always, always, ask for one of theirs because you'll need it to follow up.

5. **Don't go in with the goal of selling yourself.** I've so completely bought into the philosophy that networking is not about selling myself, that I go into every coffee meeting determined not to talk about myself at all. Maybe that sounds a little extreme, but going in with a wholehearted focus on the other person means that I'm completely engaged in their story. When I do talk about myself, it's a natural response to what's going on in the conversation or to a question; it's not me flogging my products and services. Which feels authentic and natural to me, and to the person I'm with.

6. **Arrive with an attitude of giving.** Just as I consciously plan not to speak about myself, I also make a concerted effort to identify opportunities to help my contact. Whether it's an article that relates to our discussion, or a group event I think they might be interested in, or a third-party vendor or resource I think they could benefit from knowing, I'm constantly looking for chances not only to do something nice but to continue our conversation past this single coffee date.

7. **Ask questions.** Lots of questions! Asking the right questions can keep the conversation flowing, help you uncover common interests, and build a deeper connection—which are all the reasons you set up your coffee date in the first place! Plus, asking questions shows that you're engaged and interested in their story. Showing genuine interest in your contact makes them feel valued and important. And, when you make someone feel valued and important, they like you. When someone likes you, they want to help you. See where this is going? Ask a lot of questions.

8. **Close with "What can I do to support you?"—and be prepared when they ask you the same.** Be definite and keep it simple. When someone asks me how they can help, I usually respond with "I'd love it if you could introduce me to any women entrepreneurs or business owners that you know." This is a great time to ask them if you can add them to your list to stay in touch (because I know you're not adding people to your list without their explicit written or verbal permission, right?). Reciprocate by asking them if they have a list so you can stay up to date with what they're doing.

9. **Offer to pay.** Especially if you've made the initial contact or invitation, pick up the tab. Be gracious if they decline. It's just courtesy. Plus, you can write it off as a business expense.

10. **Follow up immediately, or at least by end of business the same day.** If you've promised a resource (book title, link to an article, etc.), send it right away with a thank-you note for making time for you. If you've offered to con-

nect them with a third party, confirm that you'll follow up with a three-way email introduction. In today's connected world, it's also nice to make an online connection between them via LinkedIn.

NURTURING YOUR NETWORK

1. **Create a system for nurturing.** Having a system is key to ensuring that you're reaching out to the right people at the right time to support your objectives and goals. Include social media, personal correspondence, one-on-one connections, and other ways to remain in touch and strengthen your relationship.

2. **Schedule time for nurturing.** I have a new favorite mantra for my schedule: "The key isn't to prioritize what's on your schedule, but to schedule your priorities." BOOM! Thank you, Stephen Covey. We business owners get easily overwhelmed. Creating a system and a schedule for nurturing your network ensures that it gets done.

3. **"Spontaneously" check in with your contacts.** Whether you create a system (first week of the month, reach out to contacts A–G; second week, reach out to contacts H–J, etc.) or you just shoot out an email or text when someone crosses your mind, let your contacts know you're thinking about them. Ask them what's going on in their life or their business. Schedule a quick call to touch base or a longer coffee to really dig into what's happening with them. When you routinely touch base with someone, it's easier to ask for a resource or support because it's not coming from out of the blue. It's from a place of real relationship.

4. **Visit your network when you travel.** If you're traveling for business or for pleasure, reach out to your contacts at your destination and invite them to coffee. Don't want to spend your whole vacation doing business? Pick a day and a location, and tell your contacts you'll be there if they want to drop by and say hi. If you're attending a professional event that your contacts will also be attending, make a point of connecting with them before the event to plan a cocktail or grab lunch together during a break.

5. **Share opportunities.** This is one of my favorites. I seem to be on a million mailing lists, and I get notifications all the time of events, seminars, webinars, and resources. I regularly share networking and professional opportunities within the WEBO Network Facebook group, and I post trainings and seminars on my own coaching page. Some people ask me, "Why do you share 'competing' resources with people you're marketing to?" and I say, "Why not?" I'm positioning myself as a valuable—and generous—resource, and I believe know that comes back to me in the form of referrals, leads, and new business.

6. **Be generous with leads.** Think of your network first. There's a reason that many leads groups don't allow you to be members of more than one organization. It's because they want members to share great opportunities with other members first. Use the same approach with your network. Be on the lookout for opportunities for leads and referrals, and be generous about setting up introductions between your contacts.

7. **Send birthday greetings.** It may sound trite, but people love to be recognized. The fact that you've noted their personal details and that you're taking time to celebrate them on their most special day goes a long way in building the "like" factor.

8. **Invite them to an event.** Because I frequent different groups and events, I usually tap someone in my network to go with me. This has two purposes. First, I don't have to go alone, which soothes some of my (still prevalent) networking fears; and second, it positions me as someone who's willing to share resources. If it's an event that they didn't know about but that's right up their alley, it also positions me as an expert resource—someone who's "in the know" and worth keeping around.

9. **Share resources.** Whether it's an article, a book, an organization, or an event, share resources that your contact will find valuable to their own business. It shows that you're paying attention to what they value and what's going on in their business—and that you're there to support them.

10. **Schedule regular connects.** Time constraints may mean that you have to limit this to your top-priority connections, but nothing beats meeting in person. Sharing a coffee, a meal, or a walk in the park is a great way to build a deeper, more personal relationship with your network. I find that these are the times that I learn more about my contacts' personal lives and what's important to them, which then means I have even more opportunities to delight them with relevant resources and information.

11. **Thank them.** When someone offers up an introduction, a referral, or a lead that converts into a contract or project, go out of your way to thank them. I like to send cards and gifts that not only reflect me and my business but also the value that's correlated to the quality and financial return of the business they sent my way (e.g., more revenue = bigger thank you). And, as a plug for "looking like you have your sh*t together," consider investing in branded thank-you cards!

12. **Don't be lazy.** Nurturing your network isn't something you can put off. When you make new connections, immediately put them into your nurturing system based on their priority status. Networks and relationships atrophy without attention and care. You don't want to get down the road in your business and need support from your network, only to find that you've let it languish and that your trees are no longer bearing fruit (aaaaaand...we're back to the orchard).

13. **Maintain an abundance mentality.** In point number 5, I said I regularly share opportunities and resources that could be considered competitive with my business. I do that for a couple reasons. First and foremost, because I really believe there's enough business for all of us. Networking is all about the Law of Attraction: what we put out into the Universe is what we get back. If we're authentically meeting and connecting with others in a desire to help them succeed, if we're generously giving and sharing resources and expertise, we'll be met with the same support for our success and generosity of spirit. Give leads freely.

Make connections between your connections. Introduce everyone, share everything, support others' success. It feels great and it works.

To recap. Networking is about connecting. It's not about selling. Be specific about what your goals are—for yourself and with your connections. Be professional and prepared. Look for ways to take your new relationship beyond the first coffee. I wish someone had told me not only what to expect from networking but how to do it. That's why I'm all too happy to share these tips with you.

CONCLUSION

I wish (oh, how I wish) I could tell you that I've always been aware and purposeful and intentional with my business activities. That I oh-so-carefully plan and execute and get the exact results I want every time.

But, alas, I cannot.

I mean, I guess I could. I could tell you that ever since I completed my personal networking challenge, everything I do has gone perfectly smoothly, every group and event has yielded nothing but new business, and my bank account is overflowing. I could tell you that I've rocked the sh*t out of my networking efforts, never made a mistake, and had nothing but excellent results. But I'd be a big, fat liar.

And, I'd never lie to *you*!

Nope. The truth is, I'm still learning. Every time I attend a new event or visit a new group, I learn something new about this thing we call networking. Whether it's a new way to share my story, a new way to ask for a connection, or a new way to evaluate my results, I'm still growing my skills.

Like you (I'm assuming, since you picked up this book), I have some mindjunk around networking. Maybe those scary stories you're telling yourself are about not being good enough, or witty enough, or charming enough to network successfully. Maybe you share my fear of big, scary rooms full of not-friendly strangers.

I hope that by now you see that you can overcome those anxieties and that you can build your "networking muscle" through practice and repetition. That when you create awareness, purpose, and intent (API) around your networking, you can create systems, scripts, and strategies that help you feel in control and alleviate some of your negative emotions about it. And that when you eliminate those emotions, you can become a networking superstar.

If you take these five things away from this book, you'll make me a happy girl:

- Be aware of your objectives and goals for networking.
- Align your activities with purpose and intent—including the groups you choose and the connections you make with other people.
- Show up, be all in, and make the commitment to yourself and your business to create the consistent presence that will build the beneficial relationships you're aiming for.
- Track your investments and your results so that you can further your awareness around your efforts and have a clear view of your successes.

- Stick with it. Networking is a long game (that might be the last time I get to say that to you—*sniff*). Be patient, find a system that works for you, and give it the chance it deserves.

When our friend Bob joined that tribe all those many eons ago, he could have created strong social relationships by supporting the other members in their own survival. Being known and appreciated by even one other person in the tribe might have meant someone asking, "Where's Bob?" before the lions pounced.

Poor Bob.

Luckily today, we know that Bob was hardwired not only to join that little tribe of pre-people, but that Mother Nature also made it tough on him—the stranger among strangers—to build those vital connections.

That knowledge means that we're no longer at the mercy of our unconscious fears, but that we can be mindful and purposeful about building our social and business connections in a way that lets us survive and thrive at networking.

ACKNOWLEDGMENTS

Holy cow. I wrote a whole book! I would not have been able to do it – mentally, spiritually, logistically, or energetically without the support and love of my tribe. I hate getting sappy, but here goes. Thank you to:

My husband John. I think I confuse and confound you most of the time, but you always support and encourage my crazy schemes and dreams (you know, as long as they don't cost too much). Thank you for being my biggest cheerleader and my biggest grounding force. Forever and always, more than anything.

My two chickens, Megan and Jacob. You are my light, my heart, and my everything. 'Nuff said.

My dad, Jon McGraw, for setting the example of business ownership and being my most trusted advisor. I have always felt your love and pride. I've almost forgiven you for dragging me all over God's creation for the first 18 years of my life, because apparently (as the seven moves since then have shown) being the Professional New Girl is my destiny and not necessarily your fault. Thank you for the support and encouragement in completing my book. Now that I'm finished with mine, I promise to work on yours. I love you.

My mom Harriet, who is no longer with us but I know is watching and thinks my writing this book is pretty awesome. Miss you, mom!

Julie Fuller, for being my person. Thank you for pulling my head out of my...business...and always being up for an adventure. I hope you know how much you mean to me. Let's go get some queso when this thing is done. Julie Haman for being my first friend when I moved to Broomfield in 2011 and for being my friend today. They say that friendships that last more than seven years will last a lifetime. So very happy to be doing this life thing with you! Robbyn Fernandez for your unwavering support of this book and for your gift of friendship. I'm so glad that I made a dork out of myself when I "asked you out" to be my friend. You are a blessing to me. All of you have shown me a depth and trust in friendship that I've experienced rarely in my life, and for that I am so, so grateful. I love you all.

Lisanna Parkhurst, Paula Petrock, Ashlee Thigpen, and Julie Evans. My oldest and truest friends. Thank you for holding me in your heart and lives through my many moves. Your constancy in friendship and love has carried me through times when I was struggling to build new communities.

Deb Laflamme, my first business coach, who inspired me, encouraged me, prompted me, and kicked my ass as I struggled to get my networking game together. Without you, there would be no WEBO Network. Thank you for every good thing you brought to me and my business.

Stephanie Vinton for proving that first impressions don't always count! Thank you for being my accountability partner, my business supporter, and my friend. I look forward to many, many more Saturday mornings strategizing our way to success. Kerry Borcherding for reaching out (when neither of us loved networking) to make a connection. I'm so, so glad I pushed through the fear to attend that luncheon the day that I met both of you ladies. The Universe knew what it was doing, as always.

The other members of the WEBO Network Advisory Board, Sarah April, Haley Bartlett, Kristen Judd, and Debbie Mason, thank you for generosity of time and energy to help guide WEBO as we grow. I love what we're building and I couldn't do it without your help. Seriously, I'd spin out of control and spontaneously combust without each of your strengths, talents, and knowledge to help keep me focused. Your constant support is a gift to me. Thank you, thank you for being part of this journey.

Alexandra O'Connell, my book-coach-turned-editor, thank you for helping me stay focused and organized and moving forward to get this book done. Thank you for the grace you gave me when it languished on my desk for five months during the graduation/summer/college orientation seasons. And thank you for reassuring me as I asked again and again "but, did you learn anything???" Polly Letofsky of My Word Publishing, thank you for helping guide the process of making this book a reality. You are one cool chick for helping those of us with dreams put them on paper and share them with the world.

Laura Uzzle, Ana Bogoger, and Jill Keuth for encouraging me, lifting me up, and making me feel loved. You are my people. Kim Mattei for being one of my biggest cheerleaders and for having a heart the size of Indiana. Mary Ann DeMartin for showing me how important nurturing our networks is and how to do it with aplomb.

Cindy Goyette, Karen Christen, Kacie Morrish, Angela Alter, Destiny DeHaven, Annmarie Stasica, Brigid Jones, Kelly Haugh, Patrice Gerber, Dana Young, Ana Medina, Maureen Phillips, Jennifer Scott, Lynne Williamson, Kim Alladice, Mary Peck, Stacy Nickels, and Emily Wishall for no other reason that that you came into my life purely through networking, and that your friendships delight me, fill my heart, and make me smile.

To all the members of WEBO Network, thank you for letting me serve, for being part of my dream of creating a space for women to celebrate business ownership and grow in their professional development, and for showing up ready to share and support each other in a heart-centered, professional way.

Finally, to everyone in my network who was once a stranger, but who has welcomed me into their organization, their business, or to their table across a cup of coffee. Thank you for sharing your time and spirit. Thank you for your kindness. Thank you for helping to chip away at my fear of networking and for being part of my tribe.

NOTES

Introduction

1. Ned H. Kalin, "The Neurobiology of Fear," Scientific American 268 (May 1993): 71–81.

2. Gareth Cook, "Why We Are Wired to Connect," Scientific American, October 22, 2013, https://www.scientificamerican.com/article/why-we-are-wired-to-connect/.

3. Lynn Stuart Parramore, "The Social Death Penalty: Why Being Ostracized Hurts Even More Than Bullying," AlterNet, June 2, 2014, https://www.alternet.org/culture/social-death-penalty-why-being-ostracized-hurts-even-more-bullying.

Chapter 1

4. Nan S. Russell, "Why Don't We Trust Each Other More?" Psychology Today, October 29, 2016, https://www.psychology-today.com/blog/trust-the-new-workplace-currency/201610/why-dont-we-trust-each-other-more.

5. Andrew Gelman, "The Average American Knows How Many People?" New York Times, February 18, 2013, https://www.nytimes.com/2013/02/19/science/the-average-american-knows-how-many-people.html.

Chapter 4

6. Ivan Misner, Hazel M. Walker, and Frank J. De Raffelle Jr, Business Networking and Sex: Not What You Think (CityIrvine, CA: Entrepreneur Press, 2012), 180.

7. "3 Ways to Calculate Your Training and Development Budget" HR Insights Blog, ERC, October 18, 2018, https://www.your-erc.com/blog/post/3-ways-to-calculate-a-training-and-development-budget-for-your-organization.aspx.

Chapter 11

8. Glenn Croston, "The Thing We Fear More Than Death," Psychology Today, November 29, 2012, https://www.psychologytoday.com/blog/the-real-story-risk/201211/the-thing-we-fear-more-death.

Chapter 13

9. Amanda J. Griffin, "Name Tags and Lapel Pins: Are You Wearing Them Correctly?" U.S. Chamber of Commerce Foundation, September 3, 2013, https://institute.uschamber.com/name-tags-and-lapel-pins-are-you-wearing-them-correctly/.

10. Christopher N. Cascio, et al., "Self-Affirmation Activates Brain Systems Associated with Self-Related Processing and Reward and Is Reinforced by Future Orientation," Social Cognitive and Affective Neuroscience 11, no. 4 (April 2016): 621–629, https://academic.oup.com/scan/article/11/4/621/2375054.

11. Amy Cuddy, Presence: Bringing Your Boldest Self to Your Biggest Challenges (New York: Little, Brown and Company, 2015), 199.

12. SNL Transcripts Tonight, "Daily Affirmations with Stuart Smalley," December 14, 2002, https://snltranscripts.jt.org/02/02hsmalley.phtml.

Chapter 14

13. Maddy Osman, "28 Powerful Facebook Stats Your Brand Can't Ignore in 2018," Sprout Social, https://sproutsocial.com/insights/facebook-stats-for-marketers/.

14. "Number of 1st Level Connections of LinkedIn Users as of March 2016," Statista, accessed December 13, 2018, https://www.statista.com/statistics/264097/number-of-1st-level-connections-of-linkedin-users/.

Chapter 16

15. Ivan Misner, "The returns you receive through networking are like the apples you pick from an orchard you started from a single seed," Facebook, April 9, 2018, https://www.facebook.com/IvanMisner.BNIFounder/photos/the-returns-you-receive-through-networking-are-like-the-apples-you-pick-from-an-/10155601041997956/.

REFERENCES

Bergeron, Bryan and Daniel Sands. Information Technology in the Healthcare System of the Future. MIT Open Courseware. As taught in Spring 2009. https://ocw.mit.edu/courses/health-sciences-and-technology/hst-921-information-technology-in-the-health-care-system-of-the-future-spring-2009/.

Cascio, Christopher N., Matthew Brook O'Donnell, Francis J. Tinney, Matthew D. Lieberman, Shelley E. Taylor, Victor J. Strecher, and Emily B. Falk. " Self-Affirmation Activates Brain Systems Associated with Self-Related Processing and Reward and Is Reinforced by Future Orientation." Social Cognitive and Affective Neuroscience 11, no. 4 (April 2016): 621¬–629. https://academic.oup.com/scan/article/11/4/621/2375054.

Cook, Gareth. "Why We Are Wired to Connect." Scientific American, October 22, 2013. https://www.scientificamerican.com/article/why-we-are-wired-to-connect/.

Croston, Glenn. "The Thing We Fear More Than Death." Psychology Today, November 29, 2012. https://www.psychology-today.com/blog/the-real-story-risk/201211/the-thing-we-fear-more-death.

Cuddy, Amy. Presence: Bringing Your Boldest Self to Your Biggest Challenges. New York: Little, Brown and Company, 2015.

Gelman, Andrew. "The Average American Knows How Many People?" New York Times, February 18, 2013. https://www.nytimes.com/2013/02/19/science/the-average-american-knows-how-many-people.html.

Griffin, Amanda. "Name Tags and Lapel Pins: Are You Wearing Them Correctly?" U.S. Chamber of Commerce Foundation. September 3, 2013. https://institute.uschamber.com/name-tags-and-lapel-pins-are-you-wearing-them-correctly/.

HR Insights Blog. "3 Ways to Calculate Your Training and Development Budget." ERC. October 18, 2018. https://www.your-erc.com/blog/post/3-ways-to-calculate-a-training-and-development-budget-for-your-organization.aspx.

Kalin, Ned H. "The Neurobiology of Fear." Scientific American 268, no. 5 (May 1993): 72–81. http://people.brandeis.edu/~teu-ber/fear.pdf.

Misner, Ivan, Hazel M. Walker, and Frank J. De Raffelle Jr. Business Networking and Sex: Not What You Think. City: Entrepreneur Press, 2012.

Misner, Ivan. "The returns you receive through networking are like the apples you pick from an orchard you started from a single seed." Facebook, April 9, 2018. https://www.facebook.com/IvanMisner.BNIFounder/photos/the-returns-you-receive-through-networking-are-like-the-apples-you-pick-from-an-/10155601041997956/.

Osman, Maddy. "28 Powerful Facebook Stats Your Brand Can't Ignore in 2018." Sprout Social. https://sproutsocial.com/insights/facebook-stats-for-marketers/.

Parramore, Lynn Stuart. "The Social Death Penalty: Why Being Ostracized Hurts Even More Than Bullying." AlterNet. June 2, 2014. https://www.alternet.org/culture/social-death-penalty-why-being-ostracized-hurts-even-more-bullying.

Russell, Nan S. "Why Don't We Trust Each Other More?" Psychology Today, October 29, 2016. https://www.psychologytoday.com/blog/trust-the-new-workplace-currency/201610/why-dont-we-trust-each-other-more.

SNL Transcripts Tonight. "Daily Affirmations with Stuart Smalley." December 14, 2002. https://snltranscripts.jt.org/02/02hsmalley.phtml.

Statista. "Number of 1st Level Connections of LinkedIn Users as of March 2016." Accessed December 13, 2018. https://www.statista.com/statistics/264097/number-of-1st-level-connections-of-linkedin-users/.

ABOUT THE AUTHOR

Katherine McGraw Patterson (known widely as KP), is a business strategist, speaker, and founder of WEBO Network. KP offers clients expertise gained over 20-plus years' experience in marketing support for professional services firms. She first established an independent consulting service in Hong Kong in 1999, and after several years of success in the international market, Katherine returned to the US in 2002, where she applied this critical experience in addressing the marketing needs of small businesses. Since then, she has helped small businesses and entrepreneurs in a myriad of industries across the US, Canada, and the world develop their brands and create stunning marketing materials that attract customers and drive revenue.

KP with members of WEBO Network.

Today, KP empowers entrepreneurs and small business own-ers to transform their businesses through greater profit, greater clarity, and greater satisfaction . She uses her personal and pro-fessional experience to help bridge the gap between where you are and where you want to be by identifying a clear vision and a solid strategy to achieve proactive growth.

KP is passionate about helping business owners understand how their unique talents, brand, and ideal audience influence ev-erything they do in their business–from marketing and messag-ing, to products, pricing, and services delivery, through to net-working and how they show up in the world. She encourages her clients to operate with a clear awareness of their goals and objec-tives, so that they can be purposeful and intentional about the actions they take in their business.

Mom to Megan and Jacob, KP currently lives in Denver, CO with her husband John and dog Charlie, where she enjoys walking local trails, dabbling in art, and connecting with her community through volunteering and community service.

KP works with individual clients and owner/employ-ee teams one-on-one, and through workshops and trainings (in-person and online). To work with her in achieving your business goals, visit KatherineMcGrawPatterson.com or email KP@KatherineMcGrawPatterson.com.

A high-energy and engaging speaker, KP is available to pres-ent a number of topics to business groups and networking orga-nizations. Download a copy of her speaker's sheet or invite her to your group at KatherineMcGrawPatterson.com or email KP@ KatherineMcGrawPatterson.com.

Did you love the actionable tips and tools provided in this book? Download your copies at LunchingwithLions.com. Follow KP on social media for more useable strategies you can put to work in your business!

- Facebook.com/KatherineMcGrawPattersonLLC

- Instagram.com/BizCoachKP

- Twitter.com/BizCoachKP

- LinkedIn.com/in/KatherineMcGrawPatterson